Symbolic Defense

Symbolic Defense

The Cultural Significance of the Strategic Defense Initiative

Edward Tabor Linenthal

With a Foreword by Paul Boyer

UNIVERSITY OF ILLINOIS PRESS
Urbana and Chicago

The author gratefully acknowledges a grant-in-aid from
the Swann Foundation for Caricature and Cartoon.

This book is printed on acid-free paper.

Library of Congress Cataloging-in-Publication Data

Linenthal, Edward Tabor, 1947-
    Symbolic defense : the cultural significance of the Strategic
Defense Initiative / Edward Tabor Linenthal ; with a foreword by
Paul Boyer.
        p.   cm.
    Includes index.
    ISBN 0-252-01619-X (alk. paper)
    1. Strategic Defense Initiative—Social aspects—United States.
2. United States—Defenses. 3. United States—Politics and
government—1981- 4. United States—Civilization—1945- I. Title.
UG743.L56   1989
358'.174—dc19   88-32111
                                                         CIP

For Ulla
Minä Rakastan Sinua

Contents

Foreword

On August 8, 1945, barely forty-eight hours after an American atomic bomb had destroyed a Japanese city, Anne O'Hare McCormick wrote in the *New York Times* that the new weapon had caused "an explosion in men's minds as shattering as the obliteration of Hiroshima." Many other social observers at the dawn of the atomic age commented on the pervasive impact of the Bomb on American culture and consciousness. But for the most part, students of American intellectual and cultural history failed to follow up on this early recognition of the larger impact of nuclear weapons. They remained largely on the sidelines while political scientists documented the agonizing ambiguities of the arms control process, diplomatic historians unraveled the decision-making process that led to Hiroshima, and a new breed of "defense intellectuals" elaborated their rococo strategic doctrines.

In recent years, this has begun to change. The realization is gradually dawning that if we are fully to understand the way the Bomb has shaped social reality, we must look also at the cultural realm, from the creative arts to the mass media. The editors of the *New Boston Review* articulated this growing awareness in December 1981 when they wrote that "contemporary culture grows in a dark place, beneath the shadow of the nuclear threat." The struggle to understand and ultimately to escape this "dark place" will "not be just political. It will be cultural. Nuclear weapons, after all, are a product of our culture. . . . As artists, writers, critics, and readers, we have to recognize that our history and culture created and perfected nuclear weapons." *Symbolic Defense,* Edward Linenthal's latest foray in contemporary American cultural history, is informed by this new insight. While deepening our understanding of the nuclear debates of the Reagan years, this work also represents a case study of how a cultural perspective can illuminate the larger contours of the nuclear reality.

Initially, scholarly and journalistic discussion of the Strategic Defense Initiative (SDI) focused on its technical feasibility, its implications for the arms control process, and its effects on the Nuclear Freeze campaign of the early eighties. Linenthal is concerned with these issues, but the thrust of his brief yet highly illuminating study is somewhat different. His aim is to explore the larger cultural resonances and ramifications of the SDI debate. In offering the American people a seductive vision of a technological escape from the looming nuclear threat, he argues, the president drew upon deep cultural memories of centuries of virtual invulnerability to external attack—a period that came to a decisive end, so it seemed, in August 1945. In this sense, Linenthal suggests, SDI represents another of our periodic national efforts to regain, by semimagical means, that Edenic sense of perfect security.

From his vantage point as a scholar of American religion, Linenthal views SDI essentially as a secular "symbol of deliverance." Elaborating this insight, he offers a penetrating critique of the rhetorical strategies employed by SDI proponents: their insistence on American exceptionalism and national innocence (Who could possibly suspect virtuous America of contemplating a first-strike strategy?); their technological hubris; and their vehement attacks on deterrence doctrine (an ideology few had seen fit to challenge before SDI and the lucrative research contracts that came with it entered the picture). He also examines the way SDI champions offer visionary images of a world free from nuclear fear and how they employ a utopian New Age rhetoric that was once the exclusive vocabulary of the radical left and the peace movement. *Symbolic Defense* thus offers illuminating persectives on the ironies of American political discourse and the way a common stock of rhetorical images can be appropriated by the most divergent interest groups pursuing widely disparate political agendas.

One of Linenthal's more significant contributions is his comprehensive analysis of scores of political cartoons generated by the SDI debate. From the earliest moments of the atomic age, this medium of cultural expression has played an important role in shaping nuclear attitudes. Within days of Hiroshima, for example, political cartoon commentary on the atomic bomb both reinforced wartime racist stereotypes of the Japanese and heightened the wave of atomic fear surging across America. In the 1950s, the memorable cartoons of Herblock in the *Washington Post,* portraying the Bomb as a shambling, pinheaded giant, dwarfing statesmen, politicians, and ordinary citizens alike, graphically captured a spreading public realization that the nuclear arms race was spiraling out of control. Yet, despite the obvious importance of this medium of public discourse, students of our nuclear culture have been slow to utilize political cartoons in any but the most cursory way. Linenthal's study impressively demonstrates the nuances of meaning that can be drawn out of these ephemeral documents in the hands of a sensitive cultural historian.

I welcome the publication of *Symbolic Defense*. Its range of sources, its imaginative reading of the evidence, and its interpretive insight convincingly underscore the point made on that distant August day by Anne O'Hare McCormick: nuclear weapons have, indeed, penetrated our consciousness in ways we are only slowly coming to understand. As we examine in specific contexts the actual workings of the quasi-religious belief system that Robert Jay Lifton has called Nuclearism, we can begin to grasp the way nuclear weapons have insinuated themselves into our national life, our public discourse, and our very culture. An understanding of this process must involve not only explorations of the surface levels of strategic and technological debate but also of the shadowy, half-submerged realm of cultural imagery and deeply embedded national myths. *Symbolic Defense* makes a significant contribution to this essential undertaking.

Paul Boyer

Preface

One of the fascinating aspects of the "cultural fashion" is
that it does not matter whether the facts in question are true
or not. No amount of criticism can destroy a vogue. There
is something "religious" about this imperviousness to criticism.... But even beyond this general aspect, some cultural
fashions are extremely significant.... Their popularity...
reveals something of Western man's dissatisfactions, drives,
and nostalgias.

Mircea Eliade[1]

This book is about one of the most revealing cultural fashions of our
time, the Strategic Defense Initiative (SDI). On March 23, 1983, President Ronald Reagan reawakened the long-dormant controversy over
the promise or peril of missile defense when he asked the nation's
scientists to embark on research designed to make nuclear weapons
"impotent and obsolete." Since that day, when the president articulated
his Grand Vision, most observers have seen fit to focus solely on the
technical and strategic controversies surrounding missile defense—
whether or not, and how, it would work. We easily forget, of course,
that there is no "it"; there is only the "I" in SDI, an *appealing* vision
of a world made secure through missile defense or an *appalling* vision
of a world nearer nuclear catastrophe because of missile defense. There
has never been a *nonexistent* weapons system that has generated more
passionate veneration and contempt.

Symbolic Defense examines the struggle to define the cultural significance of SDI. Both supporters and opponents of missile defense have
understood that the real battle will be won or lost through the effective
use of public symbols; hence, to discover the cultural truth of SDI we
must look to the symbols of American technology, space, enemies, and
nuclear age morality. In the process, it becomes clear that each side—
the supporters and the opponents of SDI—has expressed irreconcilable
perceptions of the fundamental nature of the nuclear age and has articulated the contours of its nuclear worldview through conflicting symbolic interpretations.

This vision of missile defense revived primal reactions to the dangers of the nuclear age that had simmered for some time beneath the surface of American culture, only to burst forth in occasional spasms of nuclear anxiety. As Paul Boyer has shown in *By the Bomb's Early Light,* Americans responded to the existence of nuclear weapons in the immediate aftermath of Hiroshima and Nagasaki, not only through various symbolic expressions of apocalyptic fear generated by the Bomb, but also through widespread expressions of hope that a world transformed by the unlimited power of atomic energy would fulfill age-old utopian visions. Hence, at the birth of the atomic age, the Bomb was clothed with contradictory symbolic meanings that have continued to shape the mental landscape of American culture.

Apocalyptic fears and utopian hopes in the immediate postwar period engendered a variety of pronouncements regarding the correct paths to salvation from the terrors of the nuclear age. Similar pronouncements were made in the late 1970s by the Committee on the Present Danger and its most visible member, Ronald Reagan, who sought to alert Americans to the danger of the growing Soviet superiority in intercontinental ballistic missiles (ICBMs). Like the "bomber gap" of the 1950s and the "missile gap" of the early 1960s, this new gap—the Window of Vulnerability—was designed to locate Americans within the recognizable contours of the cold war world. And if the cold war was to be the general frame of reference, the lessons of Munich would provide the proper historical analogy. America was, the committee argued, in the same weakened strategic and spiritual position as Britain and France had been in during the 1930s. The nation had fallen victim to a failure of nerve engendered by post-Vietnam malaise, and only through a resuscitation of patriotic will could it find the internal fortitude to stand against the ideological challenge of the Soviet Union. Failure to do so, the committee insisted, would feed the totalitarian impulse and lead inexorably to war. Commitment to the modernization of nuclear weapons systems, a key ingredient in the committee's prescription for the nation, would not only close this dangerous window but signal a fundamental revival of the American patriotic spirit in the continuing cold war.

Those who believed that this muscular nuclear age patriotism was *itself* the real danger proposed to achieve salvation by paths that seemed more benign. In their view, nuclear war, not the Soviet Union, was the enemy, and the challenge was to reduce tensions so that all countries might rise above the archaic nationalisms of the past. Albert Einstein's famous dictum, that in the nuclear age everything had changed except humankind's "ways of thinking," was usually interpreted by members of the antinuclear movement to mean that these new ways of thinking had to do partly with correcting faulty perceptions of one's enemies. Enmity was often seen as the result of such misperceptions, which in turn gave rise to fear, which fueled the arms race. The weapons simply engendered more fear, thus provoking the vicious cycle of a never-ending race that could only end in catastrophe. The organizing symbol that brought many antinuclear seekers together was Randall Forsberg's 1982 call for a Nuclear Freeze. Forsberg believed that the superpowers should halt the "testing, production, and deployment of nuclear weapons and . . . missiles," the crucial first step "toward lessening the risk of nuclear war." For those who believed that the danger increased with each new weapon, the Nuclear Freeze became a persuasive symbol of the road to salvation.[2]

Also central to the fevered activism of the antinuclear movement of the 1980s was the belief that humankind suffered from a potentially lethal failure of the imagination. The first step toward salvation, according to psychiatrist Robert Jay Lifton, lay in "imagining the real." He argued that we were suffering from "psychic numbing," a term he first used to describe the condition of survivors of Hiroshima and Nagasaki but now was using to describe those caught in the illusion of diminished risk. To combat the nuclear menace successfully, we would have to develop acute images of the horrors of nuclear war and, once educated as to the profundity of such a potential tragedy, demand and help bring about substantive changes in the present deplorable situation. Consequently, like religious revivalists of old, antinuclear activists sought to awaken society to the threat of nuclear damnation, inspired by the apocalyptic fervor of Jonathan Schell's antinuclear classic *The Fate of the Earth,* by Australian physician Helen Caldicott's declaration that the earth suffered from the "last epidemic," and by graphic descriptions of the horrors of nuclear war that were common fare at public lectures, in university courses on nuclear weapons, and on television. The hope was that people could be scared into action, as, for example, by ABC's airing of *The Day After* on November 20, 1983.

That nuclear horror might serve as the basis for an informed body politic was evident in the creation of a symbol perfectly suited for the time: Nuclear Winter. In a 1983 article in *Science,* several scientists, including the popular Cornell professor Carl Sagan, declared that even a modest detonation of nuclear weapons would bring on an environmental catastrophe that could end life on earth. Warnings of such devastation were not new. Nevertheless, this widely publicized "evidence" was welcomed by those who thought, somewhat naively, that such a scientifically certified end-of-the-world scenario would surely jolt the superpowers to their senses, motivate them to reduce the size of their nuclear arsenals, and perhaps engender support for nuclear disarmament. Lifton, for example, spoke of Nuclear Winter as a "turning point in human consciousness."[3]

Antinuclear activists have, by and large, asked too much of their symbols, even a potent one like Nuclear Winter, which communicates radically different "truths" about the nuclear dilemma. In his testimony before a congressional committee, former Assistant Secretary of Defense Richard Perle scoffed at Sagan's suggestion that, in light of Nuclear Winter, U.S. nuclear targeting policy should be radically revised and that drastic arms reduction should begin immediately. Perle argued that the possibility of Nuclear Winter made it all the more imperative that the Reagan administration's policies be swiftly implemented. The first implication to be drawn, he said, was that "we had better assure the effectiveness of our deterrent force because, whether we like it or not, the best hope we have of preventing nuclear winter, and the other consequences short of nuclear winter that would nevertheless be devastating beyond belief, is to deter that war from ever taking place. And the policy of this administration and previous administrations is aimed at doing precisely that. . . . So first, we need to assure the effectiveness of our deterrent forces." Perle went on to argue that the administration's approach to arms control and its commitment to SDI were the best insurance against nuclear war and, consequently, Nuclear Winter.[4]

Each of these powerful symbols—the Window of Vulnerability, the Nuclear Freeze, and Nuclear Winter—occupied center stage for a brief moment during the 1980s, offering a diagnosis of and a prescription for the evils of the nuclear age. Each also utilized fear—either of the Soviet Union or of nuclear weapons—as the proper motivation for public action. For these reasons, all of the symbols may have contributed to the popularity of an even more powerful symbol of deliverance: namely, SDI. Flora Lewis of the *New York Times,* in particular, criticized antinuclear groups for their "scare tactics" and wondered if such a "fright campaign" might have brought in its wake a "mindless response." "Did the Freeze," she asked, "bring us Star Wars?"[5]

SDI combines a vision rooted in American traditions of isolation and innocence with technological optimism and a fascination with the final frontier of space. Yet it also derives its symbolic power from the contradictory perceptions of nuclear weapons that have endured since 1945. For true believers in missile defense, SDI spells promise, not fear. Descriptions of its social significance resemble the utopian pronouncements regarding the "sunny side of the atom" in the 1950s. For opponents of missile defense, SDI means an extension of nuclear terror into space, bringing the world ever closer to nuclear catastrophe. The task of SDI supporters has been to market it within these evocative cultural traditions, while its opponents must unmask such utopian hopes and reveal the dangerous seductive power of the Vision.

Symbolic Defense freezes a piece of cultural history: the formative years of the popular controversy over President Reagan's vision of missile defense. Reconstructing the life and significance of a cultural fashion is akin to an archaeologist digging through the ruins of an ancient site, trying to piece together the life of the place. In the course of my research, I have dug through the discourse of American public culture including editorial comment, transcripts of television newscasts, political rhetoric, the impassioned language of religious and secular groups that support and oppose SDI, and, most significantly, the revealing visual imagery of American editorial cartoonists. These are the modes of discourse that so greatly influence the secondhand worlds all of us live in, and it is through them that most of us come to assess the social significance of controversial cultural fashions.

ACKNOWLEDGMENTS

The research for this book was carried out during a 1986-87 sabbatical year spent as a postdoctoral fellow in the Defense and Arms Control Studies Program at the Massachusetts Institute of Technology. I owe a great deal to Arthur L. Singer, vice president of the Alfred P. Sloan Foundation, who, along with Professor Jack Ruina, director of the program at MIT, made this research fellowship possible. While I have never aspired to become what some people call a "defense intellectual," it did seem to me that working on this kind of project in the company of people who spoke the language of security studies would force me to test my analytic approaches and hypotheses with those who were concerned with the same issues but were working from quite different perspectives. I refined my understanding of this material in constant conversation with faculty and graduate students in the program, and, as a result, I am indebted to Professors Ruina, George Rathjens, Steven Meyer, Steven Miller, and Charles Glaser. Sybil Francis offered me invaluable material on pro-SDI interest groups which she had collected during her years as a congressional assistant to California Congressman George Brown. Tad Homer-Dixon and Professor Marc Trachtenberg provided food for thought during our lunchtime conversations. Bill Durch was, as always, a good friend who had valuable words of advice. My officemate, Cris Gibson, and the staff of the Center for International

Studies made my year one that I will remember fondly. MIT's Susan Bjorner offered me crucial bibliographic assistance, and staff at various Harvard and MIT libraries were always friendly and helpful.

Through the generosity of MIT's program I was able to spend a week in Washington, D.C., interviewing a number of people who helped me make sense of the cultural world of SDI: Sidney Blumenthal of the *Washington Post;* Rear Adm. Eugene Carroll, U.S. Navy (ret.), now deputy director of the Center for Defense Information (CDI); Sandford Gottlieb, also of CDI; Dr. Alan Geyer, executive director of the Churches' Center for Theology and Public Policy; Lt. Gen. Daniel O. Graham, U.S. Army (ret.), director of High Frontier, Inc.; Dr. Kim R. Holmes, James T. Hackett, and Robert Huberty of the Heritage Foundation; Professor Robert Jastrow of the George Marshall Institute; John Kwapisz, director of the Center for Peace and Freedom; Rev. William M. Lewers, C.S.C, director of the Office of International Justice and Peace at the United States Catholic Conference; Leigh Metzger of the Eagle Forum; Thomas G. Moore, past executive director of the Coalition for the Strategic Defense Initiative; Maj. Mark Rabinowitz of the Strategic Defense Initiative Organization (SDIO); Howard (Bud) Ris, executive director of the Union of Concerned Scientists, in Cambridge, Massachusetts; Edward F. Snyder, executive director of the Friends Committee on National Legislation; Jack Stevens, executive director of Citizens for America; and Professor Michael Vlahos, director of Security Studies at the Johns Hopkins Foreign Policy Institute. Thanks should also go to Betsy Antalics of the Committee for a Strong and Peaceful World; Sheila Combs of High Frontier; and Bud Ris of the Union of Concerned Scientists for allowing me access to video materials and providing me with copies of SDI advertisements that appeared on commercial television in 1985.

Elizabeth Dulany and Theresa Sears of the University of Illinois Press offered advice and assistance in numerous ways. Every author should be blessed with such support. I also owe a great debt of thanks to James Blight, the executive director of the Center for Science and International Affairs at the John F. Kennedy School of Government (Harvard University), and his wife, Janet Lang. Our first meeting was a truly serendipitous occurrence, and I look forward to projects that Jim, Janet, and I have planned together. Thanks also to Professor Paul Boyer of the University of Wisconsin at Madison, Professor Ira Chernus of the University of Colorado, Professor David Chidester of the University of Capetown and the University of California at Santa Barbara, Professor John Dower of the University of California at San Diego, Professor Dick Ringler of the University of Wisconsin at Madison, and Professor

Martin Sherwin of Tufts University, whose enthusiasm for this project helped sustain me when hours at the microfilm machine began to take their toll. Edward Stein, the secretary of the American Association of Editorial Cartoonists, gave me invaluable assistance in contacting members throughout the nation to learn of cartoons that I was not able to locate during my research. I also greatly appreciate the assistance of many of these cartoonists. And my thoughts, as always, are with the "Board of Directors."

I was able to test my interpretations through several presentations, notably those at the MIT/Harvard Summer Seminar on Nuclear Weapons and Arms Control; at the Kennedy School of Government; and, thanks to the gracious invitation of Steven E. Steiner, director of Defense Programs at the National Security Council, with the SDIO working group of the National Security Council in Washington, D.C. Portions of the material on the moral aspects of SDI appeared in "Moral Rhetoric and Moral Confusion in the Star Wars Debate," *Christian Century* (Nov. 25, 1987): 1058-61.

To my father and stepmother, who provided me with such a loving environment while my wife and children were on an extended visit to grandparents in Finland, I can only say that the memories of our year together are precious indeed. To my family, to my colleagues in the Department of Religious Studies, and to the members of the executive council of the Wisconsin Institute for the Study of War, Peace, and Global Cooperation—it's good to be home.

Introduction:
The Roots of the Grand Vision

The majority of Americans rejoiced when Japan's surrender brought an end to World War II, and many viewed the use of atomic weapons as necessary and humane: necessary, because it was thought that this fanatical enemy could only be defeated by a display of ultimate power; and humane, because many believed the Bomb saved American and Japanese lives that would have been lost in an invasion of the Japanese homelands. Yet, despite the widespread perception that the Bomb was a good weapon in a good war, the fear of the eventual vulnerability of America and even the possibility of human extinction resulting from atomic weapons pervaded American culture in the immediate postwar years. Such fears became one of the established themes of the nuclear age.[1]

This perception of vulnerability was intolerable to a people whose unique sense of world mission depended in large part on an enduring sense of the physical sanctity of the land. Whether characterized as "howling wilderness" or "New Jerusalem," theirs was an inviolable sanctuary in a dangerous world. Americans had seldom faced the same kind of desolation in warfare that other nations suffered, and this geographical good fortune was often perceived as divine sanction for the status and mission of their country. After World War II, however, the security provided by the oceans was gone, and Americans realized that they too were (or would soon be) susceptible to atomic destruction by a foreign power. More than a disquieting strategic reality, this kind of vulnerability was the ultimate form of national desecration.

Sober proclamations of this revolutionary and all-encompassing vulnerability were widespread. In the popular 1946 book *One World or None,* physicist Philip Morrison, a former member of the Manhattan Project, warned that "bombs will never again, as in Japan, come in ones or twos." Echoing Morrison's conclusion that defense was futile, physicist Louis N. Ridenour titled his contribution to that volume "There Is No Defense," for the magnitude of the Bomb made defense unthinkable. Such declarations were seconded by the most influential study of the revolutionary impact of the Bomb, *The Absolute Weapon,* in which Yale political scientist Bernard Brodie argued that "no adequate defense against the bomb exists, and the possibilities of its existence in the future are exceedingly remote."[2]

Seeking alternatives to unending vulnerability in a hostile world, contributors to early issues of the *Bulletin of the Atomic Scientists* often argued that human nature must respond creatively in order to counter the degenerative effects of the threat from the Bomb. William Higinbotham, for example, maintained that there were two paths to world security: a world government in control of atomic weapons or a continued reliance on national means of defense. The latter approach was now futile, Higinbotham declared, for "our defensive frontiers are gone." The *Bulletin* also published, approvingly, President Harry S Truman's remarks made at Fordham University on May 11, 1946, that there was "at least one defense . . . mustering this science of human relationships all over the world."[3]

In spite of the overwhelming chorus of scientific celebrities who proclaimed that the atomic age ushered in permanent vulnerability, a 1947 Social Science Research Council poll revealed widespread public optimism that the United States would eventually find a way to build defensive systems against nuclear attack: "since the scientists were able to invent the bomb, they can invent a defense. . . . The United States 'always keeps ahead.' " According to pollster Sylvia Eberhart, people had "immense faith in American science, American ingenuity, and American resources." Likewise, in 1953, J. Robert Oppenheimer, the father of the Bomb and the scientific media star of the day, still held out hope that future defenses might contribute to "some measure of an increased freedom of action."[4]

Enduring faith in American technology merged with a clarion call for all citizens to face the challenge of the atomic age with a strength and courage that would reveal the continued social relevance of the American spirit. Minority voices steadfastly proclaimed that atomic vulnerability need not and should not be accepted. In 1953, for example, *Christian Science Monitor* journalist Roland Sawyer called upon President Dwight D. Eisenhower to tell the American people in no uncertain terms how vulnerable they really were. Once apprised of the threat, Sawyer believed, Americans would make great sacrifices to meet this new atomic challenge. He drew upon storied martial images of the nation's past to ask, "Is the development of an atomic bomb any worse for those it strikes than was Pickett's charge at Gettysburg for his brave confederate soldiers?" Even if total physical defense was no longer possible, Sawyer declared, Americans would adopt a "Churchillian spirit" because patriotic enthusiasm sparked the "will to live."[5]

Certainly, fear of atomic vulnerability, faith in technology, and patriotism provided the impetus for early attempts to organize both civil defense and air defense. Civil defense sought to mobilize the American people in order to create what historian William Vandercook called the "prepared society," one that could "grin and bear it" and defeat even the atomic bomb. The narrator of a 1950 Cornell film, *Pattern for Survival,* declared: "Are we going to meet this new challenge squarely, or are we going to leave the job to someone else? Fear can be overcome only through courage, and by understanding the problems which face us as individuals and as a nation. What steps have *you* taken in your community? Have *you* joined your local Civil Defense group? . . . Have *you* taught your children how to protect themselves? . . . Have you taught them that *FEAR* is their greatest enemy? *These* are your responsibilities."[6]

Plans for civil defense emphasized physical and psychological means of limiting damage from an atomic attack, *not* how to prevent such an attack. Reports from scientific and military personnel who made up Project East River (1951) and MIT's Project Lincoln (1951-53) proved inspirational to those fortified with the American spirit who were ready to meet the challenge of atomic weapons. The ten-volume Project East River study concluded that in a war with the Soviet Union damage from atomic bombs could be kept within "manageable bounds." Among its various recommendations was the dispersal of cities as a means to prevent disruption of the economy; it also outlined ways to help survivors of atomic attack overcome psychological problems and return to normal life in the post–atomic war world.[7]

While some Americans envisioned atomic age patriotism and various "practical" programs as a way for the country to endure and survive an atomic attack, others planned for the elimination of the nation's vulnerability to attack through technological triumph. Such plans were the forerunners of SDI. Interest in ballistic missile defense (BMD) was aroused after Adolf Hitler unveiled the first ballistic missile, the V-2, during the Second World War. In 1946, the United States Air Force programs Thumper and Wizard began to explore the technical feasibility of missile defense. These efforts generated little enthusiasm because of the seemingly insurmountable technical problems. In addition, more attention was focused on the problems of creating air defense that could successfully intercept Soviet manned aircraft. Only in 1957, in response to the first test of a Soviet ballistic missile and to the national hysteria generated by the Soviets' successful launch of the satellite Sputnik, did the Eisenhower administration begin to focus on BMD.

These events, and the fresh memories of the Soviets' brutal suppression of the Hungarian uprising in 1956, heightened the sense of cold war crisis that gripped the nation. Many believed that the primary goal of the Soviet Union was the destruction of the United States, and a number of scientists warned the Eisenhower administration that the Soviet atomic threat did not lie in the distant future but, as events had shown, was already at hand. Such warnings had been expressed throughout the 1950s, usually in classified documents and confidential gatherings. The National Security Council Planning Board (1952), the von Neumann Committee (1955), and the Gaither Committee (1957) warned that the Soviets were capable of mounting a successful atomic attack and, furthermore, were well ahead of the United States in the development of ballistic missiles.

In 1958, in response to this "crisis," the Eisenhower administration created the Office of the Special Assistant to the President for Science and Technology, the President's Science Advisory Committee (PSAC), and the Advanced Research Projects Agency (ARPA). Then Secretary of Defense Neil McElroy viewed ARPA "primarily as a device for preventing uncontrolled inter-service competition in space and ballistic missile defense r&d [research and development]"; consequently, it was given jurisdiction over all BMD research. In 1958, ARPA initiated Project DEFENDER in order to carry out this research and evaluate the various chalkboard proposals for missile defense. As a part of such research, ARPA supported investigations into the role of laser weapons which might one day destroy Soviet missiles early in flight.[8]

Visions of the utility of such exotic technology generated some excitement. Spurred on by the launch of Sputnik, which symbolized the growing Soviet threat from space, Edward Teller, known popularly as the father of the hydrogen bomb, began to press for more vigorous research into the possibility of missile defense. In *The Legacy of Hiroshima,* he acknowledged the technological difficulties inherent in missile defense but added that "it would be wonderful if we could shoot down approaching missiles before they could destroy a target in the United States." Research into such defense, Teller wrote, must continue, and "if we find that we can build an adequate anti-missile defense, we certainly should." In 1962, Air Force Chief of Staff Gen. Curtis E. LeMay predicted that soon scientists would develop "directed energy weapons" that would "strike [missiles] with the speed of light."[9]

While such optimism over the immediate promise of laser weapons seemed unfounded, proponents of BMD could take heart as the Johnson administration, under heavy political pressure, decided in June 1967 to deploy a missile defense. The mission of the Sentinel program was to protect the whole country via antimissile missiles strategically housed in fifteen sites, some situated quite near large cities. It was clear, however, that such a system could not provide effective defense against the Soviet missile arsenal. Accordingly, the primary justification for the deployment of Sentinel became more modest: it would provide defense against the "Red" Chinese who had detonated an atomic weapon in that same month.[10]

Some looked with contempt at then Secretary of Defense Robert McNamara's contention that the projected threat of Chinese missiles justified the massive expense of a missile defense of questionable effectiveness. Writing in the *New Yorker,* Calvin Trillin ridiculed the plan, declaring that it brought to mind "visions of thousands of Chinese peasants laboriously carting the mud of the Yangtze to crude molds, creating out of the baked earth something that roughly resembled an intercontinental ballistic missile, straining together to pull it back on some enormous catapult, and launching it . . . to obliterate Chicago."[11] He had observed passionate opposition to antiballistic missile systems (ABM) in various communities in Illinois and noted that Chicagoans did not mind the idea of being defended but wanted it done from some other place!

Defense against ballistic missiles remained a contentious issue until the U.S.-Soviet ABM treaty, which placed severe restrictions on the development and deployment of ABM systems, was signed in April 1972. Unlike contemporary debates over SDI, opponents of ABM could focus on the unappealing prospect of having defensive missiles in their "backyards," which certainly played a large role in the vehement opposition to Sentinel. Even after this program was scrapped in 1969, during the first Nixon administration, in favor of a more modest defense of missile silos (Safeguard), public opposition continued. A number of scientists spoke out in a variety of public forums against ABM, and new acronyms characterized citizens' groups working against missile defense: SCRAM (Sentinel cities reject antimissiles, in Seattle), WOMAN (women opposed to missiles and nuclear warheads, in Detroit), and NO ABMS (Northfielders opposed to ABM systems, in Minnesota).[12]

Fascination with this earlier version of missile defense revealed cultural attitudes that would surface again after President Reagan's speech in March 1983: fear of atomic vulnerability, faith in American technology, fascination with progress in exotic technology (like the laser), and the perceived inspirational value of the patriotic spirit. These all tilled the soil for public receptivity toward Reagan's Grand Vision. While the promise of such defense during the ABM debates was not fulfilled, owing both to the technical realities and the eventual restrictions in the ABM treaty, true believers in missile defense did not give up hope that this dream would someday become reality.

Clearly, then, visions of effective missile defense did not suddenly come into being in March 1983. Yet, while long-standing uneasiness with atomic vulnerability or debates about missile defense that took place in the 1960s may have set the stage for a reawakening of interest in missile defense, this does not provide answers to two questions: why did such visions arise again; and why did this vision seem to evoke more partisan passion than *any* previous attempt at missile defense?

True believers in missile defense found a sympathetic ear in the White House when Ronald Reagan was inaugurated. During his unsuccessful campaign for the GOP nomination in 1976, he had made no secret of his long-standing dislike of the fact that the United States was susceptible to destruction by Soviet nuclear weapons and his equally long-standing fascination with missile defense—prompting David Hoffman of the *Washington Post* to conclude that "the seeds of [Reagan's] turn to strategic defense were planted in the mid-70's." During a tour of the North American Aerospace Defense Command (NORAD) in the summer of 1979, Reagan was reportedly astonished to find that there was no defense of *any* kind against enemy missiles. He told Robert Scheer of the *Los Angeles Times:* "I think the thing that struck me was the irony that here, with this great technology of ours, we can do all this yet we cannot stop any of the weapons that are coming at us. I don't think there's been a time in history when there wasn't a defense against some kind of thrust, even back in the old-fashioned days when we had coast artillery that would stop invading ships if they came."[13]

As a movie actor, Reagan had been acquainted with futuristic visions of exotic technologies that could shoot things out of the sky. In a 1940 Warner Brothers film, *Murder in the Air,* he starred as FBI agent Brass Bancroft, whose mission was to apprehend a spy who was attempting to steal an "inertia projector." Bancroft described the weapon as "a device for throwing electrical waves capable of paralyzing alternate and direct currents at their source. Remember that news story that broke some time ago and was hushed up about the amateur radio operator in Kansas who was stopping automobiles and streetcars and electrical appliances for miles around with some sort of radio beam?" Well, Bancroft told his friend, a large-scale version of that technology was to be tested as a combat weapon. The admiral in charge of the project declared that, if successful, the impact could be revolutionary: "Yes, Doctor, and wait 'till you see it in action. It not only makes the United

States invincible in war, but in so doing promises to become the greatest force for world peace ever discovered, which is the hope and prayer of all thinking people, regardless of race, creed, or government." Eventually, of course, Bancroft used the "inertia projector" to bring down a plane carrying the enemy spy.[14]

A quarter of a century after his role in this film, Reagan was caught up in the possibility of making such cinematic fantasy a reality. In 1967, sixteen years before he offered his Grand Vision to the nation, he talked about the prospects for missile defense with Edward Teller at Lawrence Livermore National Laboratory. Teller was then, as now, an enthusiastic advocate of missile defense, arguing that it was necessary because the United States was "more open to a sudden attack than Poland was in 1939."[15]

As a result of such experiences, when Reagan began his 1980 campaign for the presidency, he was receptive to suggestions from friends like Teller that the time was right to announce a "new way of thinking" about the dilemmas of the nuclear age. During the early stages of the campaign, Martin Anderson, his domestic advisor, wrote a defense policy memorandum that gave Reagan an option of publicly endorsing research into a "protective missile system." Anderson recommended that the policy should become known as " 'Reagan's Peace Plan' or some such nomenclature." At the same time, the alarmist rhetoric of the Republican party platform called for "vigorous research and development of an effective anti-ballistic missile system, such as is already at hand in the Soviet Union." For political reasons, the plan was not used during the campaign; but, in retrospect, it is clear that interest in the potential of missile defense was building.[16]

Although Teller has proudly claimed that he was responsible for convincing the future president that missile defense was an idea whose time had come, there were other significant actors in the drama. One influential voice belonged to Lt. Gen. Daniel O. Graham (ret.), a former head of the Defense Intelligence Agency and founder of High Frontier, Inc., a missile defense advocacy organization. Graham had been interested in missile defense since the mid-1970s, and after trying unsuccessfully to interest the American Security Council in his plans, he found a home for his "high frontier" concept at the Heritage Foundation. In March 1982 he published the first of a series of High Frontier studies that claimed "a global ballistic missile defense system is well within our present technological capabilities and can be deployed in space in this decade." While often at odds with other missile defense enthusiasts, who favored more exotic technologies over his plans to destroy missiles with high-velocity projectiles, Graham claimed that he and his supporters "went public in March 1982 and by March 1983 we had the President of the United States going our way."[17]

Reagan was going their way for other reasons as well. Joining Teller in support of missile defense were three old friends of the president: brewer Joseph Coors, oilman William Wilson, and businessman Karl Bendetsen, a former under secretary of the army. Beginning in the summer of 1981, these four members of Reagan's "kitchen cabinet" met several times with the president and a group of missile defense advocates at the Heritage Foundation to discuss the possibilities. All of them were apparently optimistic about Teller's pet project, the X-ray laser (Excalibur). On January 8, 1982, the "kitchen cabinet" met with Reagan to advocate a more vigorous research program.

Excitement about other exotic technologies that could play a role in missile defense also reached the president. One group that favored chemical lasers based in space included Sen. Malcolm Wallop (R., Wyo.), Sen. Harrison Schmidt (R., N.M.), and Rep. Ken Kramer (R., Colo.), who had been influenced by aerospace engineer and space enthusiast Maxwell Hunter's 1978 pamphlet, "Strategic Dynamics and Space Laser Weapons." After reading it Wallop exclaimed, "By God, we're going to do something to defend this country!"[18] To this end, beginning in 1980 he fought successfully for increases in funding for the development of space-based laser missile defense.

All these diverse strands of interest set the stage for a climactic meeting between the president and the Joint Chiefs of Staff on February 11, 1983. Reagan spoke of his interest in missile defense and was supported by the chairman, Gen. John Vessey, and the naval chief of staff, Adm. James D. Watkins. Watkins, a Roman Catholic, was reportedly deeply influenced by early drafts of the American Catholic bishops' 1983 pastoral letter, "The Challenge of Peace: God's Promise and Our Response." He and former Deputy National Security Advisor Robert McFarlane argued for missile defense as a "moral imperative" and asked a question that would make its way into the Grand Vision speech six weeks later: "Wouldn't it be better to save lives than avenge them?" When the president was questioned about the importance of this meeting, he recalled that the Joint Chiefs were enthusiastic, and he remembered asking them: "Isn't it possible that with our modern technology and all that we have been able to develop, that it would be worthwhile to see if we could not develop a weapon that could perhaps take out, as they left their silos, those nuclear missiles? And the Joint Chiefs said that such an idea . . . was worth researching." Then, the president said, "I gave the order—I said 'Go.' "[19]

Certainly, these voices of support were crucial in the formation of the president's vision of missile defense, but Reagan was far from being a passive observer. Unlike any other president, he began to view missile defense as more than a technological issue. He saw it as a test of whether patriotic renewal had, in fact, invigorated the nation to take bold initiatives that would shake off the final vestiges of the lingering malaise of the Vietnam era. Whereas, during the earlier ABM debates, Richard Nixon could say that every "instinct motivates me to provide the American people with complete protection, . . . [yet] it is not within our power to do so," Ronald Reagan, similarly motivated, believed that *anything* could be done by Americans who had the will to overcome illusory limits. The challenge posed by missile defense, in Reagan's view, was primarily a problem of national will, not technology. For the president, SDI was an example of the creative promise of a "Second American Revolution," which he called for in his State of the Union Address on February 6, 1985. "There are no constraints on the human mind . . . no barriers to our progress," he said, "except those we ourselves erect."[20]

This vision of missile defense—what would eventually become known as SDI—was perceived by the president as having both restorative and transformative power. Through it, technological achievement in the present would bring about the resurrection of an Edenic past. Reagan's vision became a crucial element in the program of cultural restoration of the New Right, for it promised to bring to life the peaceful, secure, "Main Street" America whose passing he had decried. It would restore an invulnerability that would, in turn, allow the nation to chart its own destiny; it would transform the nature of international conflict and promised, eventually, to bring within reach the vast riches of space. As a *Washington Post* editorial noted, the Grand Vision speech, delivered on March 23, 1983, brought together the diverse strands of interest in ballistic missile defense "in a form that caught the public's attention." The plan seemed both appealing and revolutionary to a public unfamiliar with the history of ballistic missile defense and uncomfortable with what appeared to be the increased risk of nuclear war. Certainly, it was this particular vision of missile defense, one designed to make the nation invulnerable, that captured the imagination of many.[21]

The Grand Vision was introduced in the midst of feverish public engagement with a variety of nuclear anxieties. From within a cauldron of anti-Soviet enthusiasm, technological exuberance, continuing attacks on the strategic status quo from both left and right, and discussion by officials in the Reagan administration about fighting and winning nuclear war, the president seemed to offer the nation new hope. The immediate context of the speech revealed the tumult of the time. Only fifteen days earlier, Reagan had spoken to the National Association of

Evangelicals and characterized the Soviet Union as the "focus of evil" in the world. He also had criticized the Nuclear Freeze as a "dangerous fraud, . . . merely the illusion of peace." On April 4, the Challenger shuttle was launched for the first time. On May 3, the National Conference of Catholic Bishops released its celebrated pastoral letter which criticized nuclear deterrence as a long-term strategy for peace and claimed that such deterrence could only serve as a temporary condition while the superpowers moved toward arms reductions. Earlier drafts of the letter had been widely circulated, prompting the Reagan administration to press the bishops to portray its policy in a favorable light. Even before publication, however, the bishops' message was viewed as an endorsement of the Nuclear Freeze, which the House of Representatives also endorsed on May 4. On September 1, the Soviet Union shot down a civilian jet liner, an act perceived by many as the true mark of an evil empire. On November 14, the first cruise missiles arrived in England, amid strident anti-American protests throughout Europe. On November 20, over 100 million Americans watched nuclear war in ABC's *The Day After.* And on November 23 and December 8, respectively, the Soviet Union withdrew from the Intermediate Nuclear Forces (INF) talks and the Strategic Arms Reductions talks (START).

The Grand Vision portion of the president's address to the nation was an add-on to a speech that urged public support for an increase in defense spending—an increase made necessary, according to the president, because of the growing Soviet threat. It was within this ominous context of a renewed cold war that Reagan talked about missile defense and "new hope for our children in the 21st century," despite what seemed like an eternity of nuclear vulnerability. He expressed a yearning that transcended ideological boundaries and spoke directly to the nuclear anxieties of the moment. The president declared his disdain for the "spectre" of mutual threat, concluding that it was a "sad commentary on the human condition." He was "convinced" that "the human spirit must be capable of rising above dealing with other nations and human beings by threatening their existence." Then Reagan turned to the nation's scientists, "those who gave us nuclear weapons," and challenged them to apply the same seemingly miraculous powers to "give us the means of rendering these nuclear weapons impotent and obsolete" and thereby achieve world peace. "Tonight," he noted, "we're launching an effort which holds the promise of changing the course of human history."[22]

The impact of the speech illustrated the power of presidential words. In his stinging criticism of the Grand Vision, former Under Secretary of State George Ball remarked that such words were to be used only with "scrupulous restraint"—which was not evident in the speech and certainly would not have contributed to the power of the message. The president offered the Grand Vision during a time when fears of the Bomb had led to a cultural despair that, despite the wishes of anyone, deterrence was eventually bound to fail, resulting in a nuclear catastrophe. Those more worried about the Soviet Union than about nuclear war were convinced that the United States was forgetting the lessons of Munich, which were still relevant in the nuclear age: namely, that appeasement of an insatiable aggressor would inadvertently invite Soviet aggression, which in turn might lead to a nuclear war. Reagan's speech held out hope to people of various ideological persuasions that the same scientists who had burdened humankind with nuclear weapons could now, motivated by patriotic fervor and blessed with seemingly God-like technological genius, provide the only sure path to salvation—the path of missile defense.[23]

1

Veneration and Contempt: Response to the Grand Vision

Immediately following President Reagan's Grand Vision speech on March 23, 1983, CBS news anchor Dan Rather asked state department reporter Bob Schieffer for his reaction to the plea for missile defense. Said Schieffer, "I don't think it's going to generate even very much comment." He could not have been more inaccurate, for the public and private response has been both prolific and passionate, with supporters and opponents battling to interpret the Vision.[1]

Many people shared the president's conviction that missile defense could change the course of human history. Reagan's science advisor, George Keyworth, who only learned of the speech a few days before it was delivered, was reportedly "surprised, shocked, and stunned" by its content. Yet he became a passionate supporter of missile defense and, almost two years after the speech, exclaimed, "In March 1983, Ronald Reagan changed the course of twentieth century Man." Reverential pronouncements were also made by a surprised and delighted Edward Teller, who reassured readers of the *New York Times* that the president did indeed have a good grasp of missile defense. In their meetings together, Teller noted, the president had wanted to know "a vast number of details" about the practicalities of missile defense. Now, like Winston Churchill and Franklin D. Roosevelt, Reagan's courageous action "may save us from a future war and provide the needed basis for peace."[2]

Two days after the speech the *Wall Street Journal* offered its support of the idea, declaring that missile defense would allow the nation to "control our own destiny if we have the will and the courage to do so." In March 1984, Sen. Pete Wilson (R., Calif.) called the speech a "turning point in American history" and said he was quite sure that even a "modest research program" could solve most uncertainties within five years. University of California at Berkeley historian Walter McDougall, author of . . . *The Heavens and the Earth,* argued that missile defense signaled substantive changes in the nature of the nuclear world. Writing in the *National Review,* he envisioned offensive nuclear weapons gradually becoming extinct, with missile defense then inaugurating a new age: "The last historical purpose of the retaliatory doctrine could be to shelter the transition to a new, mature nuclear age launched in space."[3]

While McDougall and others understood missile defense as part of a cultural transformation of long duration, others were excited about the more immediate benefits. Daniel Graham's High Frontier, Inc., one of the most influential advocacy groups, believed that missile defense need not wait on long-term research, that it could be done here and now. Members were asked to think about the urgency of such a defense in light of the horrors of ABC's *The Day After.* The group's November 1983 newsletter carried the headline, "ABC's 'The Day After' Could Be Prevented by High Frontier."[4]

Some commentators gave more cautious support to the idea of missile defense. William Safire thought that the president was using good common sense by "lurching forward to a new era in arms control." The *Detroit News* questioned whether the administration was "beset by unilateralists and those who would profit electorally from the 'peace' movement"; such enemies might, in fact, sabotage efforts to bring the Grand Vision to life. Others simply expressed their frustration at the current dangerous situation between the superpowers. Perhaps missile defense *was* unrealistic, wrote *Newsweek*'s Meg Greenfield, but could anyone really feel "intellectually or morally content" with a deterrent policy that required the nation to be ready to "obliterate millions upon millions of innocent, helpless, human beings"? She saw the president's vision as a useful reminder of the poverty of present strategic doctrine, and she thought that even if missile defense was not the answer, it might serve as a welcome tonic to prod the "status quo gang" to "think radically."[5]

Opponents of missile defense greeted the speech with fierce criticism, attacking the Vision from every conceivable angle. Appearing on a March 30, 1983, "CBS News Special Report: The President's Defense Policy: Other Views," George Rathjens, professor of political science at MIT and former chief scientist and deputy director of the Advanced Research Projects Agency (ARPA), spoke of the illusory promise of space defenses and characterized the Grand Vision as "cruel and irresponsible, like a physician offering laetrile to patients afflicted with cancer." DePaul political scientist Patrick Callahan spoke of missile defense as a "delusion" and offered his opinions about the contentious issues that would be debated in the coming years: defense would have to be perfect in order to bring about a truly transformed world, the costs would be enormous, the Soviets would develop effective countermeasures, and testing would eventually violate the ABM treaty. "The delusion of defense," he wrote, "is the ultimate danger."[6]

Angry editorials appeared in many newspapers. Describing the Vision as "The Death-Ray Solution," the *Chicago Tribune* declared on March 26, 1983, "What better, more exhilarating, more *American* way out of the nuclear dilemma than to build Pac-Man weapons. . . . Warp speed, Mr. Spock!" On April 4, 1983, the *Atlanta Constitution* brought its readers a Russell Baker column chiding the president for his "Space Wars" speech. Unlike other chief executives who had to deal with the harsh realities of the nuclear age, Baker believed that Reagan thought only of the "next century filled with deadly space gadgets constructed for struggle against the 'Evil Empire' of communism." The *St. Louis Post-Dispatch* claimed that the instability brought about by missile defense would heighten the danger between the superpowers. "This," the editors declared, "is not Star Wars, this is madness." The *New York Times* warned in December 1983 that "To Act on This Dream Portends a Nightmare." Editors at the *Los Angeles Times* perceived the Vision as the product of a quirky tinkerer, a "crackpot scheme," like the abortive nuclear-powered planes of the 1950s or the congressional decree for a cure for cancer in 1976. A final indignity was heaped upon the president and the speech when Art Buchwald portrayed Reagan's old movie friend, Bonzo the chimpanzee, instructing a gullible president in the wonders of missile defense.[7]

Differing reactions to the speech also came in the important struggles between opponents and supporters to assign an appropriate name to the president's vision. Boston College sociologist William A. Gamson objected to "Strategic Defense Initiative" because, he argued, it communicated images of defense that were nothing more than "soothing anodynes" to nuclear vulnerability. The editors of the *New York Times* agreed. Even the use of the word "initiative," they thought, had the ring of "nationalism, of aspiration, of boldness." In Gamson's view, "Star Wars" conveyed the accurate message that the cold war was being extended into space. Names mattered, said Gamson, because in accepting certain names we "inadvertently accept a whole package, hidden assumptions and all."[8] Both supporters and opponents fully understood that since missile defense remained, at least for the present, only a vision, public support or opposition would be shaped less by "facts" than by persuasive images and symbols. The naming struggles were a sign of the broader battles that were to come.

Richard Sellers, co-founder of the Coalition for the Strategic Defense Initiative, an umbrella organization associated with High Frontier, Inc., that coordinated support for SDI among numerous grass-roots groups, blamed Sen. Edward Kennedy (D., Mass.) for characterizing the Grand Vision as "Star Wars" (after George Lucas's 1977 film) on the floor of the Senate the day after the speech. Sellers argued that "Star Wars" implied "hostilities and death and . . . a fictional capability that's in the Hollywood realm and can't be done"; but, he added, SDI "can be done." *Boston Globe* reporter David Wilson insisted that, over a year before the president's speech, *he* first popularized the term in a 1982 article on a High Frontier conference he had attended: "High Frontier is Star Wars, nature imitating art." Even before Wilson, however, a 1980 issue of *Mother Jones* carried an article warning about the coming threat of weapons in space, entitled "No Need for Star Wars."[9]

Reagan, too, was sensitive about the name. Asked in 1985 if he objected to the term "Star Wars" being used to describe the Vision, he replied that he did, because it was "first used in an effort to denigrate the whole idea." It had, Reagan thought, the "sound of an image of destruction back and forth," and he cautioned that it was important to remember that missile defense was meant to destroy weapons and not people. Some of the president's most ardent supporters, however, thought that "Star Wars" was appropriate. For example, Phyllis Schlafly of the Eagle Forum argued that Reagan's Vision, like the movie, was a "drama of the battle between good and evil, and of the triumphs of good over evil through adventure, courage, and confrontation." Other supporters were more concerned about the name chosen in 1984 to describe both the Grand Vision and the organization that would try to bring it about: the Strategic Defense Initiative, or SDI. Jack Stevens, executive director of Citizens for America, the president's grass-roots lobby, said, "We like to call the plan the space shield." And in the latter months of 1984 and into 1985, Reagan occasionally referred to his vision as the "Peace Shield."[10]

Unhappy with all these names, William Safire reminded readers of the *New York Times Magazine* of the utility of good acronyms. He sympathized with the president's dislike of "Star Wars" but said he was not enamored with SDI and was not moved by some of the other names that had been suggested: Study of Protection (STOP), Security Assured for Each (SAFE), and Mutual Assured Safety (MAS), a presidential suggestion. In the early months of 1985, Safire asked his "nuclear happy" readers to submit suitable acronyms in order to reach "arms control immortality." One month later he reported over 600 responses. Opponents weighed in with predictable derisive fare: Ballistic Offensive Neutralization Zone and Bulwark Order Negating Zealous Offensive (BONZO); Defensive Umbrella (DUMB); Wistful Attempts to Circumvent Killing Ourselves (WACKO); and Western Intercontinental Missile Protection (WIMP). Proponents, of course, offered acronyms that communicated quite different messages: Defense of Outer Space (DEUS);

Security against Nuclear Extinction and Shield against Nuclear Extermination (SANE); Shield against Fatal Encounter (SAFE); Defense in Space against Russian Missiles (DISARM); Hostile Projectile Elimination (HOPE); and Defense Oriented Missile Employment (DOME).[11] For opponents of missile defense, such comforting but misleading names and acronyms were further examples of "nukespeak," language that seductively increased the gap between a word and the thing that word was supposed to represent. Referring to "defensive" space weapons was, according to opponents, one way to diminish the human imaginative power to understand and respond to the real danger of such weapons.

Many of the nation's editorial cartoonists reacted negatively to the president's speech. Draper Hill of the *Detroit News,* whose later cartoons supported the Grand Vision, offered the sobering image of a tiny president with a whip attempting to tame the ubiquitous symbol of the postwar world, the nuclear genie who mocks a pathetic attempt to escape from the nuclear age. Doug Marlette of the *Atlanta Constitution* and Paul Conrad of the *Los Angeles Times* ridiculed the Grand Vision using the familiar image of the emperor with no clothes, and Don Wright of the *Miami News* and Jeff McNelly of the *Chicago Tribune* mocked the Vision as an exercise in silly fascination with technological "toys." Wright, Marlette, Jack Ohman of the *Oregonian,* Linda Boileau of the *Frankfort State Journal,* Jimmy Margulies of the *Houston Post,* Tony Auth of the *Philadelphia Inquirer,* and Jim Morin of the *Miami Herald* all portrayed the crazy scheme of a president lost in science-fiction fantasies of wars in space.

Some cartoonists characterized Reagan as a befuddled technological tinkerer. One week after the speech, David Seavey offered his version in *USA Today* of the origins of the Vision: after the president read *National Geographic* and saw the cover picture of a frog extending its tongue to catch a bug, his inspiration was born. Dick Locher of the *Chicago Tribune* and Auth characterized the president as a technological infant, blissfully unaware of the dangers of the toys he was playing with. Others immediately picked up on the comparisons to the heroes and villains of the *Star Wars* movies. Steve Kelley of the *San Diego Union* showed the president surrounded by the "crack team of experts" that included R2D2, C3PO, and, from another film, ET. Paul Szep of the *Boston Globe* portrayed Reagan as the villain Darth Vader, while Ohman suggested some different names for the Vision, and Boileau characterized SDI as a form of nukespeak.

YOU GOTTA BE KIDDING, FELLA

Reprinted with the permission of Draper Hill and the *Detroit News.*

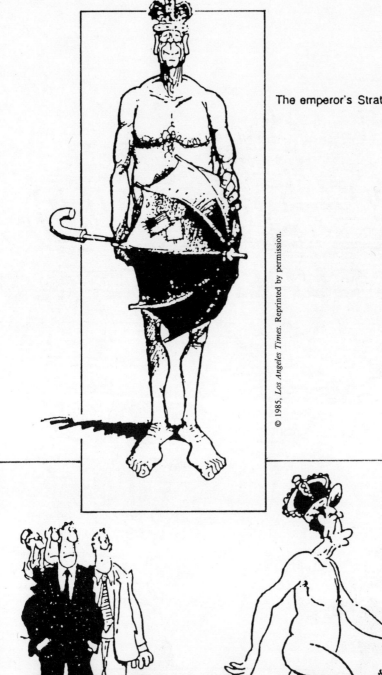

The emperor's Strategic Defense Initiative

" THE EMPEROR HAS NON-EXISTENT DEFENSE TECHNOLOGY!.. "

BUCK RONALD
AND HIS SUPER LASER GUN

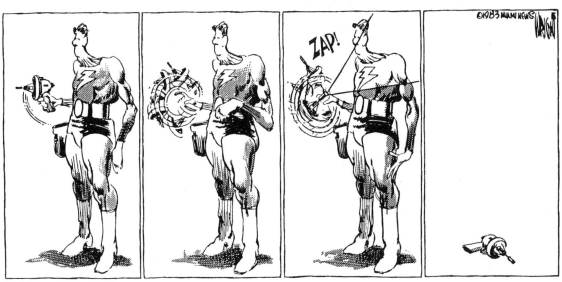

Reprinted with the permission of Don Wright and the *Miami News*.

HOW STAR WARS WILL WORK

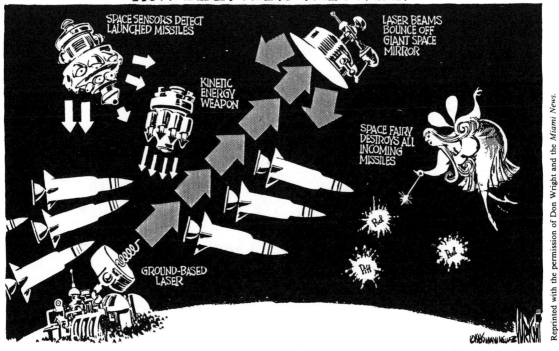

Reprinted with the permission of Don Wright and the *Miami News*.

Reprinted with the permission of Doug Marlette.

'Earth to Ron! . . . Earth to Ron!'

Reprinted with the permission of Jimmy Margulies and the *Houston Post.*

S.D.I·in·the·sky.

Reprinted with the permission of David Seavey and *USA Today.*

26   *Symbolic Defense*

Reprinted by permission of Steve Kelley and the *San Diego Union*.

Reprinted courtesy of the *Boston Globe*.

'Really, Ronnie, sometimes I honestly think there's more
to life than Star Wars and a Soviet arms buildup.'

28 *Symbolic Defense*

Linda Boileau, *Frankfort State Journal*—ROTHCO.

The president's speech also sparked a bitter public debate among many of the nation's scientists; and, like the SDI program, the debate grew slowly but inexorably in scope. On January 6, 1984, Reagan signed National Security Decision Directive 119 (NSDD-119), which officially created the Strategic Defense Initiative; the actual organization (SDIO) designed to coordinate a wide variety of research programs was formed on March 27, 1984, and on April 4, 1984, Lt. Gen. James Abrahamson was named its director. Also in April, the Office of Technology Assessment (OTA) published its evaluation of the prospects for missile defense. *Directed Energy Missile Defense in Space* concluded that, inasmuch as there was only a "remote" chance that any form of missile defense could protect the nation from "mortal" damage, such hopes "should not serve as the basis of public expectation or national policy." The report, written by Ashton Carter, assistant director of the Center for Science and International Affairs at the Kennedy School of Government (Harvard University) was immediately attacked. SDIO disagreed with the conclusions, and Daniel Graham of High Frontier, Inc., resigned from the OTA advisory panel because he objected not only to the report's conclusions but also to what he saw as the covert influence on the report of "anti-SDI experts" whose reputations were made by enshrining Mutual Assured Destruction (MAD) decades ago. Tom Wicker of the *New York Times* praised the report, as did the editors of the *St. Louis Post-Dispatch,* who characterized it as a "report to heed." The controversy was so fierce that OTA's director, John Gibbons, had to appoint a three-person panel to review the report, but even their stamp of approval did not satisfy those who saw it as the opening salvo in the official war to kill SDI.[12]

The OTA report was followed in October 1984 by *The Fallacy of Star Wars,* a book by the Union of Concerned Scientists (UCS). Founded in 1969 to "encourage a more humane use of scientific and technical knowledge," UCS was in the forefront of resistance to the development of missile defense. The book sparked angry reaction from SDI enthusiasts, who accused the members of UCS of being radical ideologues, hiding behind the pretense of scientific objectivity. After the 1984 elections, the *Wall Street Journal* argued that the president's popularity clearly showed that the public supported SDI and had rejected "flawed" arguments against it from opponents like UCS. In any case, sniffed the *Journal,* the UCS book could "hardly be called science." Others also made UCS the object of their wrath. Writing in a High Frontier newsletter, William Rusher characterized the group as a "miniscule clutch of leftists with a hyperactive xerox machine." The *National Review* called the book "specious and ideologically tainted" and declared that the group had been a "scandal for years—a letterhead with a few distinguished names acting as shils for a membership of left-wing laymen."[13]

This vehement reaction to the OTA and UCS publications bore witness to the influence of both. Editorial writers in newspapers across the nation often cited the OTA report, and *The Fallacy of Star Wars* provided grist for the mill of many grass-roots opponents of SDI. No popular text appeared from a scientist supporting SDI until Robert Jastrow, professor of earth sciences at Dartmouth College and founder of NASA's Institute for Space Studies, published *How to Make Nuclear Weapons Obsolete* in 1985. Enlarging upon arguments made in several *Commentary* articles the year before, Jastrow concluded that the weight of established scientific opinion would eventually support SDI because it was clearly a feasible project. He claimed that anti-SDI scientists either were consciously manipulating data to make SDI appear more difficult than it really was or had been subliminally influenced by their liberal political views and, consequently, were not aware that they were really engaged in politicized science. In any case, Jastrow argued, most scientists who opposed SDI had not had any experience in evaluating defense technologies; hence, their reactions to SDI were invalid. He saved much of his venom for IBM physicist Richard Garwin, a longtime, influential opponent of missile defense who had been active in the Union of Concerned Scientists and had contributed to their published attacks on SDI. Throughout 1984 and 1985, Garwin and Jastrow carried on lengthy and complicated print debates, full of bitter personal invective.[14]

Besides the burgeoning popular "scientific" debates over the merits of SDI, the president's speech kindled a renewal of scientists' activism of a kind not seen since the ABM debates of the Johnson-Nixon years. In the Grand Vision speech, Reagan had asked scientists to respond to the challenge of missile defense with the spirit that had infused the Manhattan Project. Then, on February 12, 1985, the president invited seventy-five leading scientists, including twenty-two Nobel Laureates, to a White House dinner, at which he asked them to look forward to SDI research with "vision and hope." That same spring, a letter went out from SDIO to a wide range of university scientists encouraging them to enlist in SDI research in the "new and exciting time for us in the science and engineering community." To the displeasure of SDIO, however, scientists on many of the nation's campuses generally greeted this invitation with hostility. University of Illinois physicist John Kogut, for example, who helped organize scientific opposition to SDI, thought that the "program could not survive the light of free discussion."[15]

Scientists, in particular, were displeased with SDI for a variety of reasons. In addition to questioning the wisdom of the program, many feared that participating in SDI research would restrict academic freedom and "blur the distinction between classified and unclassified research." From such concerns came the "Pledge of Non-Participation," born on May 16, 1985, at the University of Illinois at Urbana-Champaign and in June 1985 at Cornell University; a joint pledge to resist the temptation to do SDI research began circulating on campuses in September 1985. The pledge called SDI "ill-conceived and dangerous," not "technically feasible," and declared that even a partial defense would be a "step toward the type of weapons and strategy likely to trigger a nuclear holocaust." Scientists who signed the pledge hoped to "persuade the public and Congress not to support this deeply misguided and dangerous program." Also in May 1985, UCS released an appeal to President Reagan and Soviet Premier Mikhail Gorbachev, signed by over 700 members of the National Academy of Sciences, to ban space weapons. Adding fuel to the controversy were angry denials from the presidents of the California Institute of Technology and MIT to the claim made by the director of SDIO that both schools had decided to participate in SDI research. In his June 1985 commmencement speech, MIT President Paul Gray accused SDIO of using the school in a "manipulative effort to garner implicit institutional endorsement."[16]

Despite this vehement, articulate, and widespread opposition to SDI, official optimism detected a quite different spirit on the nation's campuses. In July 1985, James Ionson, director of SDIO's Office of Innovative Science and Technology, declared that "virtually everyone, on every campus, wants to get involved." Shortly before that, the *Wall Street Journal*'s Gregory Fossedal wrote that there was a "broad emergence—in some cases a shift" in favor of SDI among the nation's scientists. Apparently oblivious to widespread scientific opposition and activism, Fossedal misinformed his readers by telling them that a technical consensus existed among the nation's scientists. Even after 6,500 signatures opposing SDI research had been gathered, Ionson declared that a boycott "would not have any impact on the program whatsoever." In fact, he claimed, SDIO had received far more unsolicited research proposals than it could fund. At the same time, Martin J. Hoffert, chairman of New York University's Department of Applied Science, told the *Washington Times* that there was "considerable support for the SDI program within the academic community, much more than is generally conveyed by the media." Robert Herman, a research associate at UCS responded, "That's not true." There was, he thought, no "silent majority out there who's supportive of Star Wars."[17]

Enthusiasts believed that opposition to SDI derived, for the most part, from the machinations of a left-wing conspiracy. Karl O'Lessker, a senior research fellow at the conservative Hudson Institute, thought that the anti-SDI scientists' objectives were "suspiciously well orchestrated," another example of the "unrivaled organizing abilities of the left." He worried that the public would not be able to filter out criticism of SDI because it did not know that statements by physicists, always the "most leftward leaning of all university professors," should be ignored. John Hughes, a former assistant secretary of state during Reagan's first term in office, thought scientists' protests against SDI violated the "can-do spirit" of America. Such scientific defeatism, he said, was a negation of "confident American ingenuity that has taken us to the moon and provided other technological breakthroughs." To counter such defeatism, and to show the public that there was scientific support for SDI, the Science and Engineering Committee for a Secure World was formed on May 9, 1986. Chairman Frederick Seitz, past president of the National Academy of Sciences, and eighty other scientists and engineers who supported SDI declared that technical advances had made such defenses feasible and that SDI should not be "hastily, unscientifically, or ideologically rejected."[18]

Despite official optimism about university participation, a 1986 report on the status of the research boycott stated that "over 3700 Science and Engineering professors and senior researchers have pledged not to participate in Star Wars research, as have over 2800 graduate students and junior researchers." Clearly, many of the nation's scientists took "extraordinary steps to stop what they [viewed] as an extraordinarily dangerous program."[19]

Editorial cartoonists also publicized the SDI debate among scientists. Linda Boileau, Tony Auth, and Ken Alexander characterized SDI as "hot air," "garbage," and the product of a sorcerer's brew. Jim Morin captured the despair of many scientists who viewed SDI as an example of presidential ignorance. While enthusiasts argued that anti-SDI scientists had let their liberal political persuasion distort their scientific judgment, cartoonists Auth, Joel Pett of the *Lexington Herald-Leader,* Bill Plympton, Herblock of the *Washington Post,* and Tom Toles of the *Buffalo News* raised the possibility that pro-SDI scientists were being seduced by large government research grants and painting a much too optimistic picture of the possibilities of missile defense. Chuck Asay of the *Colorado Springs Sun* took issue with the rigid skepticism that dismissed SDI too quickly, and he joined in the chorus of denunciation of the Union of Concerned Scientists.

Linda Boileau, *Frankfort State Journal*—ROTHCO.

Reprinted with the permission of Ken Alexander.

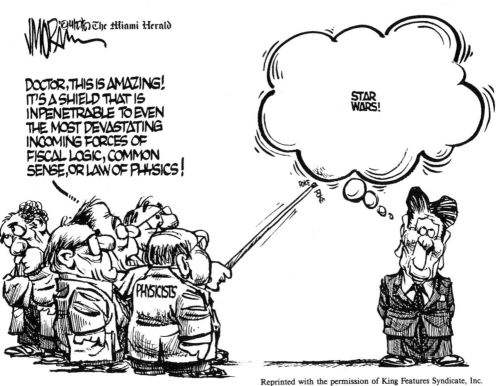

Reprinted with the permission of King Features Syndicate, Inc.

Reprinted with the permission of Joel Pett and the *Lexington Herald-Leader*.

Reprinted with the permission of Bill Plympton.

LABORATORY EXPERIMENT

"Laboratory Experiment." From *Herblock at Large* (New York: Pantheon Books, 1987).

Reprinted with the permission of Chuck Asay and the *Colorado Springs Gazette Telegraph*.

THE SCIENTIFIC METHOD:

1. STATE THE PROBLEM.

2. FORM THE HYPOTHESIS

3. OBSERVE AND EXPERIMENT.

4. INTERPRET THE DATA.

5. DRAW CONCLUSIONS.

THE UNION OF CONCERNED SCIENTIST'S METHOD:

1. DRAW CONCLUSIONS.

Reprinted with the permission of Chuck Asay and the *Colorado Springs Sun*.

During the ABM debates in the Johnson-Nixon years, the weight of scientific opposition clearly contributed to the gradual loss of official and popular enthusiasm for missile defense, but this does not seem to have happened during the SDI debates. Perhaps because the reemergence of the popular appeal of missile defense began with a presidential pronouncement from an extraordinarily popular president; or perhaps because the dangers of the nuclear age were perceived as being too acute; or perhaps because there were some scientific voices raised in support of SDI—whatever the case, scientific opposition to SDI failed to halt or even significantly stem grass-roots support for the program. Both sides chose their respective scientific "champions," who argued for their respective cases, and accused the other side of being guilty of politicized science. Hence, there was no single authoritative scientific voice from which Americans could find out the truth about SDI. Supporters and opponents alike realized that the battle would not be won solely on the weight of scientific authority but also by persuasive argument as to the social significance of SDI. The ensuing struggle was spirited, often bitter, and took place in a public environment somewhat sympathetic to the idea of missile defense. The Grand Vision speech brought into focus two fundamental and irreconcilable views of the nuclear age that had simmered beneath the surface since the temporary resolution of the ABM debates during the Johnson-Nixon years. The public was at once uninformed about the history of missile defense and ambivalent about SDI. Supporters and opponents correctly surmised that the public was waiting to be convinced either that SDI was the result of a new way of thinking in the nuclear age, which would lead to a safer world, or that SDI was a dangerous, unrealistic attempt to avoid dealing with the harsh realities of the age.

2

Restoration and Transformation: The Ideology of Strategic Defense

Political analyst Kevin Phillips remarked that the popularity of the Strategic Defense Initiative was due largely to the success of SDI enthusiasts in scoring a series of "image achievements."[1] Symbols of conquest—of past frontiers and past technological challenges—pointed to the possibility of conquering the final frontier. Symbols of fear—that the Soviets were ahead in missile defense and that an "SDI gap" was developing—pointed to the necessity of such conquest. Symbols of purity and transformation—that SDI not only represented a morally superior response to the dilemmas of the nuclear age but would usher in a *new* age—pointed to the desirability of such conquest. These images were expressed in an articulate strategic defense ideology, the heart of which was a faith fueled by the fervor of the president's Grand Vision: namely, the United States need not remain vulnerable to nuclear destruction. Liberation from the "illusion" of vulnerability would be the first step toward a rejuvenated nation, followed by the restoration of invulnerability. SDI, of course, would be the agent of restoration.

Strategic defense ideology took direct aim at the doctrine of Mutual Assured Destruction (MAD), which promised to maintain the peace by threatening unacceptable damage to any enemy who would launch a nuclear attack upon the United States. SDI supporters argued that it was not only immoral and strategically unsound (since the United States was, in their view, militarily inferior to the Soviet Union) but also unnecessary to live in a state of nuclear terror. According to strategic defense ideology, mutual vulnerability was only a "theory" that had gained legitimacy through decades of short-sighted decisions made by liberal arms controllers. High Frontier's 1982 "Proposed Statement of U.S. Policy" claimed that MAD need not be passed on to America's children; rather, the nation had a "historic, but fleeting opportunity to take destiny into its own hands." It was possible to escape from this vulnerability, which, in Daniel Graham's words, had inflicted "disastrous psychological consequences," because of the priceless legacy of American "superiority in space technology."[2]

According to some SDI supporters, there had been previous opportunities to escape from the nuclear age, but liberal conspirators had always managed to sustain the illusion that each of the superpowers must remain vulnerable in order to maintain peace. Graham joined Phyllis Schlafly, of the Eagle Forum, conservative columnist William Rusher, and Rep. Newt Gingrich (R., Ga.) in constructing this conspiracy theory. Schlafly argued that MAD grew out of liberal defeatism that began with the postwar thought of George Kennan, who, along with others, argued for the necessity of coexistence with the Soviet Union and consequently developed a "paralyzing dread of death by nuclear incineration." Out of this will-weakening attitude grew the perversion of MAD. Rusher and Gingrich claimed that liberals then learned to make good political use of MAD, providing a framework of fear within which the liberal welfare state, dependent on an illusion of limits, could flourish. SDI, however, was a "dagger at the heart of the liberal welfare state" and, according to Gingrich, "destroy[ed] the liberal myth of scarcity. . . . The only limits left [were] the limits of a free people's ingenuity, daring, and courage." Because of the promise of SDI, declared Rusher in the right-wing version of "The Times They Are A-Changin'," liberals would soon see the "carefully constructed chamber of horrors in which you mistakenly concluded mankind was doomed to live forever . . . collapsing around your ears."[3]

It was, of course, these same liberal arms control conspirators who waged spirited campaigns against SDI and incurred the wrath of SDI enthusiasts. An editorial in the *Detroit News* commented that SDI was such a good idea that "only a defense intellectual or a political scientist could be arrogant enough to deride it." Those experts from past administrations who argued passionately against SDI—Robert McNamara and McGeorge Bundy, for example—could be dismissed, noted presidential science advisor George Keyworth, because their arguments represented only the "bitter sniping from those who have failed in the past." For some, the MAD/SDI debate even became a question of basic patriotism. In 1986, William Buckley accused those who opposed SDI of "doing the work of the Soviet Union."[4]

If the political will could be found, SDI supporters were confident that America would be able to conquer the frontier of space and render Soviet missiles useless. A striking image of this conquest was Alexander Hunter's drawing that accompanied an article on the morality of SDI by Lewis Lehrman in *Policy Review:* an American eagle swooping down on incoming missiles, ready to pluck them out of space.

According to Michael Smith, professor of history at the University of California at Davis, SDI as a space program symbolized a national

44   *Symbolic Defense*

purpose that "equated technological preeminence with military, ideological, and cultural supremacy." SDI would be the most significant conquest yet on the frontier of space, and memories of old frontiers were useful in pointing the way. In his commencement speech at the Air Force Academy on May 30, 1984, President Reagan told the assembled cadets that by accepting the challenge of space, the nation would exhibit the "bold vision" of Western pioneers. High Frontier, Inc., also used this symbol, perhaps nowhere quite so graphically as in a drawing in Graham's *The Case for Space Defense,* in which a coonskin-capped Western pioneer and an astronaut merge.[5]

The pioneer tradition—that "bold vision" that led generations of courageous Americans to conquer the wilderness and would lead them to conquer space—also served to provide a redemptive sacrificial framework for the technological tragedy that threatened public confidence in the inexorable march of American technology. In response to the Challenger disaster of January 28, 1986, the president declared, "We're still only pioneers" and such tragedies will always be a part of the "process of exploration and discovery." In a speech to a conservative political action group, Reagan stated that the disaster would only strengthen the resolve of Americans to "pursue their dream of 'the stars and beyond.' "[6]

The conquest of space through SDI was often perceived as breaking the bonds of a nuclear age fatalism that, according to some, engendered feelings of personal impotence and victimization. President Reagan was appealing to the attractive idea of self-reliance in the nuclear age when he asked, in a July 1986 radio broadcast, "Isn't it time to put our survival back under our own control?" SDI advocacy groups subsequently appealed to politicians to find the will and the funds to support missile defense, which promised an escape from the nuclear age. In one of its newsletters, for example, Citizens for America proclaimed that the country could "leave the threat of MAD behind" and develop a "peaceful, secure shield over the nation."[7] It asked its members to write to their senators and plead with them not to leave the nation defenseless.

In addition to interpreting SDI as the latest example of American self-reliance, the shapers of strategic defense ideology framed the Grand Vision within the myth of American innocence, envisioning SDI as a benevolent creation designed for the good of the world. According to this nuclear age myth, our enemies *knew* that American military forces, including SDI, would never be used aggressively; consequently, objections to the program by its adversaries were merely ploys designed to weaken domestic support. Appearing on NBC's "Meet the Press" on March 27, 1983, only four days after the Vision was shared with the

Reprinted with the permission of High Frontier, Inc.

SENATOR, PLEASE DON'T LEAVE US DEFENSELESS

The United States is now *completely defenseless* from nuclear attack. President Reagan wants to build a *nonnuclear* defensive shield to protect the country—The Strategic Defense Initiative (SDI).

The U.S. House of Representatives has *slashed* funding for SDI. This weak commitment to defense against Soviet nuclear weapons threatens to gut the President's plan. Meanwhile, the Soviets are spending 15 times this amount on their own space defense program.

The President's SDI bill is now before the Senate. PLEASE CALL YOUR SENATORS AND URGE THEM TO SUPPORT FULL FUNDING FOR AMERICA'S ONLY DEFENSE AGAINST SOVIET NUCLEAR WEAPONS—SDI.

PLEASE CALL OR WRITE YOUR SENATOR TODAY.

Reprinted with the permission of Citizens for America.

public, Secretary of Defense Caspar Weinberger exemplified this strain of American innocence:

> Secretary of Defense Weinberger: The other reason why they [Soviets] have no need to worry is that they know perfectly well that we will never launch a first strike on the Soviet Union. . . .
>
> Marvin Kalb, NBC News: Mr. Secretary, but do you understand that the Soviet Union could think, in its own planning, that the United States, and this Administration particularly, is seeking a first-strike capability?
>
> Weinberger: No, I don't see any way in which they could think that. . . . there is no basis in that thought.

In a similar vein, Richard Sybert, Weinberger's assistant, responded angrily to a suggestion by *Los Angeles Times* reporter Robert Scheer that SDI could be used as offensive weaponry. Sybert called that a "masterpiece of disinformation" and reminded Scheer that "offense and aggression are not the American way."[8]

A number of pro-SDI editorial cartoonists helped to shape the strategic defense ideology by taking direct aim at MAD. Chuck Asay, for example, in "A Primer on Modern Day Defense Strategies," illustrated the problems with MAD, a unilateral and bilateral freeze, and the SDI solution. He also took aim at the father of MAD, Robert McNamara, echoing the Reaganite conviction that since the mid-1970s the Soviet Union's nuclear buildup and its supposedly extensive civil defense program, coupled with the "unilateral disarmament" of the United States, had reduced mutual assured destruction to the assured destruction of only the United States. Asay told us that "conceptual dinosaurs" like McNamara harbored dangerous illusions about the Soviet Union and were blind to the perils of strategic inferiority.

The acronym MAD had always been an ironic one. While it was supposed to describe the conditions under which strategic stability was possible, it had come to symbolize the degraded human condition in the nuclear age. For example, cartoonist Mike Shelton of the *Orange County Register* illustrated the rabid condition of the superpowers living under the shadow of imminent destruction—which could only be prevented by SDI.

The need to escape from the madness of MAD was all the more necessary, according to SDI supporters, because destruction would no longer be mutual. The Soviet Union was capable of delivering a devastating blow to the United States without fear of effective retaliation and, further, was moving ahead in defensive weapons technology. Of course, this kind of alarmist rhetoric, which became an important part

Reprinted with the permission of Chuck Asay and the *Colorado Springs Sun.*

Reprinted with the permission of Chuck Asay and the *Colorado Springs Sun.*

The alternative to SDI is MAD.

CATASTROPHIC ILLNESS

INSURANCE

of the strategic defense ideology, was a replay of dire warnings made during the ABM debates of the Johnson-Nixon years. In 1967, for example, a Republican National Committee background paper stated that the Soviets were years ahead of the United States in missile defense; and in 1969, the American Security Council declared that ABM was still the "soundest insurance for peace and against war that the United States [could] buy . . . for the 1970s."[9]

Similar warnings permeated discussions of the need for SDI. In an April 8, 1984, edition of ABC's "This Week with David Brinkley," President Reagan informed viewers that the Soviet Union was ahead of the United States in space weaponry; indeed, the Soviets "already [had] in place such a weapon." The *Wall Street Journal* called the threat "Red Star Wars," and in the *Reader's Digest,* Ralph K. Bennett described the "Red Shield" as giving the Soviet Union the "ability to launch a nuclear first-strike without fear of effective retaliation." *Defense Watch* readers learned of the Soviets' "Dark Star," and popular television evangelist D. James Kennedy, pastor of Coral Ridge Presbyterian Church in Fort Lauderdale, Florida, warned that the United States only started work on defense in 1985, while the "Soviets [had] a massive defense around Moscow," which would "probably be left standing in case of an attack."[10]

Grass-roots advocacy groups also publicized the danger of the "SDI gap." The Coalition for the Strategic Defense Initiative and Citizens for America warned of the malevolent intentions of the Soviets and the strength of their missile defense. Concerned Women for America, a conservative evangelical organization, told readers of its newsletter that Soviet advances in missile defense had allowed them to disable American satellites with lasers. Citizens for America informed its members that SDI was necessary to counter the Soviets' "fully operational defensive shield," which would be in place "by the 1990's." Failure to respond in kind would mean "our capitulation as a free people."[11]

Editorial cartoonists also dramatized the imagined Soviet threat. For example, Mike Shelton's "Soviet 'Star Peace' " offered a graphic look at what might happen if the Soviets triumphed in the realm of missile defense: namely, the whole world would become a Soviet prison camp. Jerry Barnett of the *Indianapolis News* used the image of the evil "Death Star" from the movie *Star Wars* to illustrate the tiny U.S. research program compared to the huge Soviet program. Dick Locher employed the familiar image of the Russian bear to point out the Soviets' voracious appetite for arms and the mosquitolike impact of SDI on this buildup.

Pro-SDI cartoonists Barnett, Steve Kelley, and Chuck Asay took aim at what they considered the hypocrisy of the Soviet Union: the Russians criticized SDI as destabilizing yet moved forward with their own active program aimed at eventual deployment of a missile defense system. So, too, Soviet deployment of provocative offensive missiles had "forced" the United States to move in the direction of missile defense. Draper Hill and Dick Szep used the image of the bear to call attention to the seeming contradiction between the Soviets' self-righteous anger at SDI and their aggressive actions in Afghanistan.

As for the Soviets' position on SDI, Hill offered a parody on "The Other Day upon a Stair," while Asay argued that SDI was the crucial ingredient in bringing the Russians back to the arms control table. However, Asay warned against using SDI as a bargaining chip with the Soviets and noted how frustrated the Soviet bear was when SDI "got away" at the summit meeting in Iceland. Shelton portrayed a vindicated president, and Mike Peters of the *Dayton Daily News* turned the table to characterize Andrei Gromyko as Darth Vader. Finally, Asay, Hill, and Szep joined Bill Garner of the *Washington Times* in echoing William Buckley's belief that opponents of SDI were, at best, unwitting "dupes" of the Soviet Union.

According to strategic defense ideology, capitulation to the Soviets could only be avoided by turning to one of the recognizable strengths of the nation: namely, technological achievement. SDI was perceived by many as the latest in a long line of difficult but achievable technological projects. Rep. Ken Kramer (R., Colo.) called SDI a "Manhattan Project for Peace" and asked people to think about it in the same triumphant terms they thought about the herculean project that resulted in the atomic bomb. Caspar Weinberger remarked that, just as skeptics criticized SDI, there were those who had scoffed at the attempt to reach the moon: "Fortunately, we had President Kennedy... who took the position that this not only could but should be done. And a very few years later, we did it. So I don't have any real doubts of the American ability to do this [SDI]." Comforting comparisons also appeared in letters to the editors of various newspapers. For example, a letter in the *Christian Science Monitor* on December 10, 1985, called attention to instances where the "can't do" spirit from a "gaggle of scientists" was eventually proved wrong; and the writer believed that this naysaying spirit would also be proved wrong in the case of SDI.[12]

Comparisons with past scientific achievements were urged on legislators who would cast votes on the future of the SDI program in Congress, as in a 1986 House Republican study committee report that used the scientific controversies surrounding the development of the hydrogen bomb to frame the SDI debate. Those scientists who took a "purely" scientific approach to the bomb (Edward Teller, for example) were

SOVIET 'STAR PEACE'

Reprinted by permission: Tribune Media Services.

Reprinted with the permission of Steve Kelley and the *San Diego Union.*

Courtesy of the *Indianapolis News*.

Reprinted with the permission of Chuck Asay and the *Colorado Springs Sun*.

Reprinted with the permission of Draper Hill and the *Detroit News.*

Reprinted courtesy of the *Boston Globe.*

"To counter the sinister plans of 'Star Wars,' the USSR is putting before the international community a concept of 'Star Peace'."

— Soviet Foreign Minister Shevardnadze

Reprinted with the permission of Draper Hill and the *Detroit News*.

Reprinted with the permission of Chuck Asay and the *Colorado Springs Sun*.

Restoration and Transformation   59

Reprinted with the permission of Draper Hill and the *Detroit News.*

Reprinted with the permission of Chuck Asay and the *Colorado Springs Gazette Telegraph.*

Reprinted courtesy of the *Boston Globe.*

Reprinted with the permission of Bill Garner and the *Washington Times.*

Restoration and Transformation   61

confident that it "could and should be developed," whereas J. Robert Oppenheimer and others argued against the bomb for political reasons, although they camouflaged their objections in the language of science. This same split existed over SDI, according to the report. "Pure science" had proved that SDI was just as achievable as was the hydrogen bomb. Yet those who thought that SDI should not be brought into being were trying to "form rationalizations for why it [could not] be done."[13]

Symbols of technological "miracles" in space were used to support arguments for SDI. In April 1984, for example, shortly before taking over as director of the SDIO, James Abrahamson appeared on ABC's "This Week with David Brinkley" and reminded viewers that the triumph of the space shuttle was "ample visual evidence of those miracles." He added that there were other miracles "in the weapons systems and in the people . . . behind the technology." On the same show, Caspar Weinberger exuded confidence: "I think it can work. I don't have any doubt about it. . . . What it takes, however, is a commitment." Later, at the first symposium of the U.S. Space Foundation, Abrahamson declared that a commitment to SDI would not be in vain and certainly did not represent technological arrogance. SDI was not "unfounded audacity" but "well founded on the competence and creativity of free Americans." The editors of the *National Security Record* argued that such a commitment would also mean eventual victory in the conflict with the Soviet Union because, despite the fact that the Soviets were ahead in space weaponry, they did not have "the national energy needed to undertake a project as new and daring as the development of a high-tech strategic defense."[14]

Bill Mauldin's cartoon in the *Chicago Sun-Times* echoed a popular argument by SDI supporters: that there must be some truth in the optimistic claims about SDI or else why would the Russians be so worried about it. The organizers of High Frontier, Inc., continued to insist that missile defense could be accomplished with "off-the-shelf" technology. Norman Podhoretz, the influential editor of *Commentary*, believed that space-based defenses were "well within the reach of the United States," and his optimism was supported by some members of the scientific community.[15]

Lowell Wood, Edward Teller's protégé at Lawrence Livermore National Laboratory, one of the two federal facilities charged with the design of nuclear weapons, addressed a conference on space weapons in Sicily and argued that the problem was solely a financial one: with one trillion dollars there could be a "protective shield that would cover the entire territory of the United States." At a 1985 Heritage Foundation conference on missile defense, Wood claimed that significant defense

would be possible in "a half decade . . . [and] effectively in full-scale operation within a decade." The pro-SDI Science and Engineering Committee for a Secure World also heightened hopes for missile defense, claiming that technological breakthroughs had "significantly increased the prospect that the U.S. can successfully devise effective systems which will destroy attacking Soviet missiles."[16]

Such optimism led to the attribution of almost magical powers to missile defense. Robert Jastrow claimed that there were *no* countermeasures the Soviets could take to combat a neutral particle beam, one of the exotic technologies under consideration that would make "the Soviet missile arsenal useless." D. James Kennedy, swept away by his evangelical fervor for SDI, rhapsodized about laser weapons capable of destroying 1,000 missiles per second, and he predicted that by the early 1990s the United States would have a "system fully operational that would bring an end to the nuclear age."[17]

Supporters pointed to success in weapons tests as tangible evidence that the technology needed to bring about the new age was fast approaching. Reaction to the June 10, 1984, Homing Overlay Experiment, in which a missile pursued and destroyed a dummy warhead 100 miles above the earth, revealed this sense of excitement. Under the headline "Star Wars Works," the *Wall Street Journal* informed its readers that, "had the missile been real, one million lives might have been saved." The editors of *Forbes* declared, "Last month the nature of weapons on this planet began to change." Even investigative reporter Jack Anderson understood the test as a "momentous event" that signaled "the possibility of being able to prevent the accidental annihilation of any part of America."[18]

Further weapons tests were conducted to build public confidence; in fact, even the acronyms for some of the tests communicated this official optimism. For example, an experiment to bounce a laser off a space shuttle in June 1985 was called BEACON (Bold Experiments to Advance Confidence), while the destruction of a stationary missile in March 1985 was accomplished by a laser called MIRACL (Mid-Infrared Advanced Chemical Laser). By July 1986, a House Republican study committee felt confident enough to report that "strategic defense has progressed to the point of *how* it can best be done, not *whether* it can be done."[19]

Supporters of the strategic defense ideology who grafted nostalgic memories of the challenges of past frontiers onto American fascination with space also called attention to the ultimate importance of this frontier by utilizing familiar and effective cold war rhetoric. In the midst of an intense period of nuclear anxiety, Americans heard a cacophony of optimistic voices from the White House, from conservative think tanks and advocacy groups, and from the pulpits of certain churches. Much of this rhetoric was, of course, both mistaken and irresponsible. The Soviet Union *did* have sophisticated air defense and *did* have an energetic missile defense program, but it did not, as President Reagan proclaimed, "have in place" sophisticated and effective ballistic missile defense. Yet, when mixed with often misleading optimism about the possibilities of missile defense, such alarmist rhetoric was effective.[20]

While concern over the Soviet threat in space and excitement about supposed technological breakthroughs were making news, SDI enthusiasts sought to recapture the moral high ground from the peace movement. Throughout the nuclear age, response to Einstein's call for "new ways of thinking" usually came from those who viewed nuclear war as the ultimate threat and thus proposed various programs designed to rid the world of nuclear weapons through disarmament or some form of world government. Those who viewed the Soviet Union as the real menace could only continue to call for eternal vigilance through nuclear deterrence in an endless cold war. Nuclear weapons, in this view, were themselves symbols of deliverance from the forces of evil. SDI supporters argued that the Grand Vision was the only proper response to Einstein's challenge; hence, even as they agreed with members of the antinuclear movement that nuclear war *was* the ultimate threat, they maintained that the cold war would continue. In their view, SDI would restore principled response to endless superpower conflict in the nuclear age.

Prior to March 23, 1983, when the president delivered his Grand Vision speech, few SDI enthusiasts had publicly declared their moral qualms about deterrence. The fact that the delicate balance of terror was maintained by threatening the lives of millions of Russians had never engendered the same moral outrage among them as it had among antinuclear activists. Deterrence, conservatives argued, had "worked" for over forty years, and if the United States could keep pace with the Soviet nuclear buildup, there was no reason why deterrence would not continue to work. But deterrence would be weakened by the Soviet Union's supposed quest for nuclear superiority and by criticisms of deterrence from the antinuclear movement.[21]

The Grand Vision speech brought about a striking transformation in conservative rhetoric. Sounding like members of the antinuclear movement, for which they previously had voiced nothing but contempt, some SDI enthusiasts began attacking deterrence as an immoral national strategy that might lead to the tragic, needless death of millions of innocent Soviet citizens. Whereas before the speech utopian visions of a denuclearized world were found mainly among certain segments of the antinuclear movement, after the speech SDI enthusiasts began utilizing these same visions, which they once criticized as hopelessly naive. For them, SDI became the only realistic and benign path to salvation in the nuclear age. Stephen Rosenfeld of the *Washington Post* noted this dramatic change in rhetoric, suggesting that the president's speech took "weapons that do not exist and that we may never have . . . and arrive[d] at a place . . . previously considered the exclusive property of the left fringe."[22]

The ideology of strategic defense offered the nation a moral alternative to both deterrence and disarmament. This third path of missile defense, wrote Barry Smernoff in the *Air University Review,* "would put emphasis on preserving both life and other fundamental values." He characterized SDI proponents as "new abolitionists" who "preach against the immorality of nuclear deterrence and nuclear war." Clearly, part of the appeal of SDI was its apparently incontrovertible moral clarity, captured in the simplistic slogan "SDI will destroy weapons, not people." An early attempt to codify such sentiment was Rep. Ken Kramer's People Protection Act of May 1983, which called for protection through missile defense. Advocates of SDI claimed that missile defense would allow America to return to the "moral" principles of defense, that it would, according to Caspar Weinberger, express the "best characteristics of democratic principles." Progress in SDI technology was not only a strategic imperative but a "visionary moral quest." Lewis Lehrman claimed that SDI would restore to the president the ability to carry out his oath of office to "preserve, protect and defend the U.S."[23]

Conservative Christian groups expressed their faith in the "benevolent" technology of SDI and claimed that missile defense would restore Christian principles to the nation's defensive policy. The Coalition for the Strategic Defense Initiative announced that over 2,000 priests, ministers, and rabbis had signed its "Clergy Statement," which declared that "no nation has the right to renounce its duty to defend its people against unjust aggression." Since SDI did not pose any "threat to human life," it was "morally obligatory for the American people and their government." The Religious Coalition for a Moral Defense Policy, a coalition of conservative Protestant, Catholic, and Jewish groups, issued a statement in support of SDI on February 4, 1986, calling it the "only moral strategic nuclear military policy." The National Association of Evangelicals' "Peace, Freedom, and Security Studies" declared that SDI would not only restore a moral defense policy but could "provide the occasion for new efforts at mutual security arrangements."[24]

Conservative Catholics interpreted SDI as a direct response to critiques of deterrence in the American Catholic bishops' 1983 pastoral letter. Hans Mark, former technological adviser to the president and later chancellor of the University of Texas, believed that the bishops' criticism of deterrence was a motivating factor behind the Grand Vision speech. The president's sensitivity to the bishops' critique revealed, according to Mark, that he "is really a soft touch. . . . he's not a tough guy like Harry Truman was." Writing in *This World,* Joseph Martino argued that since SDI raised no problem of immoral intentions, it was the way out of the "perverse logic" of deterrence. Likewise, in *Catholicism and Crisis,* Kenneth Kemp declared that SDI more adequately reflected the values and vision of the kingdom of God than did either disarmament or deterrence. Both George Weigel's *Tranquillitas Ordinis* and Philip Lawler's *The Ultimate Weapon* expressed pro-SDI Catholic sentiment. For Lawler, especially, the moral case for SDI was so clear that he wrote, "If a system could be devised, American Catholics should support it!"[25]

In his widely circulated sermon "Surviving the Nuclear Age," D. James Kennedy told the biblical story of Nehemiah rebuilding the wall around Jerusalem and declared that "we need to pray that the wall around America may be built again." The same call appeared in the newsletter of conservative evangelical Beverly La Haye's Concerned

Women for America. Amid pleas to protest legalized abortion, support a revival of religion on college campuses, and see that Central American "freedom fighters" got supplies, the newsletter expressed the hope that America would " 'rebuild the wall' of our national defense" and offered a prayer for a "space shield . . . functioning as soon as possible." Both President Reagan and Thomas Moore, former executive director of the Coalition for the Strategic Defense Initiative, drew support for SDI from Luke 11:21: "If a strong man shall keep his house well guarded, he shall live in peace."[26]

In the face of such moral clarity, some SDI enthusiasts found it hard to understand any opposition. Speaking at Tufts University, the secretary of defense said that he was "baffled" that the "idea of defending . . . one's notion of the good should cause such an ethical dilemma." Weinberger blamed opposition to SDI on a "liberal" moral relativism that denied the importance of defending the values of Western civilization. This, mixed with dangerous innocence about the Soviet threat, created unwarranted qualms about SDI. But, he added, "we have created the freest, most prosperous and strongest nation in the history of the world. We have a moral obligation to defend it—and we will." An argument was also made from the morality of intention *and* consequences: that is, because the motives for SDI were life-affirming and because SDI would bring about a more secure world, there were simply no legitimate moral objections to be made about the program.[27]

Strategic defense ideology offered reassuring images of a restored and renewed America. The population, once freed from the debilitating fear of nuclear vulnerability, could return to prenuclear security by conquering the final frontier of space. In essence, SDI would take the nation back by taking it forward. Hence, images of restoration and renewal were fortified by images of transformation. Thus, in the face of criticism that population defense simply was not possible, that the most the nation could do was protect some missile silos, Reagan, Weinberger, and a few other SDI enthusiasts staunchly held out for its eventual certainty. At the very worst, there would be a gradual evolution to the total security of the American population; and an incremental deployment of SDI would represent the stages of this evolutionary process. In March 1984, the editors of the *Wall Street Journal* referred to these intermediate steps as a "technological bridge to more perfect ones." Strategic analyst and SDI supporter Colin Gray spoke of the final stages of this evolutionary process as a "truly radical, benign restructuring of strategic forces through the arms control process."[28]

Bringing SDI into being would, some thought, reveal "new ways of thinking" that were foreign to the pre-SDI world. The celebrated offer by the president to share SDI technology with the Soviet Union was scoffed at by many but hailed by others as a harbinger of the open relations that would exist in a world transformed by missile defense. Armand Hammer, president of Occidental Petroleum and an unofficial adviser on U.S.-Soviet relations to many administrations, remarked that the offer would "erect an umbrella of good will over the superpowers beneath which peace would flourish." In early 1986, Jacob Javits, New York's former Republican senator, said that such cooperation would "ameliorate the crisis atmosphere that still exists between the two countries."[29]

For SDI enthusiasts, this umbrella of good will would signify not only a safer world but a world transformed by the material treasures that space had to offer. In his 1985 State of the Union Address, the president spoke of SDI as the catalyst for a national space program that would bring with it an unrivaled prosperity. "In the zero gravity of space," Reagan exclaimed, the nation would witness the creation of "technologies and medical breakthroughs beyond anything we ever dreamed possible." In a similar vein, Harvard political economist Robert Reich portrayed a world transformed by the technological impetus of SDI: "The technology used to create X-ray laser weapons could be applied to super-microscopes; the know-how garnered in designing particle accelerators could be applied to irradiating food products. Spinoffs and applications as yet unimaginable could create whole new generations of telecommunications and computer-related products that could underpin information processing systems in the next century."[30]

This rhetoric of transformation in strategic defense ideology sounded, in fact, like that of some New Age thinkers, those who expected that dramatic events would bring about sweeping transformations in human consciousness which would in turn revolutionize human relationships. Certainly, many SDI enthusiasts perceived the Grand Vision speech as a portentous "event" for those who had ears to hear and eyes to see. Yet the often unstated belief that missile defense would usher in fundamental transformations in the way the superpowers viewed each other betrayed a deeper, unexamined assumption that SDI would profoundly influence human nature for the better. Such thinking even affected longtime supporters of missile defense like Edward Teller, who wrote in *Better a Shield Than a Sword:* "Defensive arms by themselves will not furnish insurance against war, nor will they terminate the arms race. But to the extent that the arms race is won by instruments of defense, *the psychological conditions required for international cooperation and for developing the foundations of real peace will be approached*" (emphasis mine).[31]

Proponents of missile defense have utilized strategic defense ideology to "domesticate" SDI by associating it with evocative images of past American frontiers, by portraying space as the final frontier to conquer, and by linking the progress of SDI technology to the promise of a fundamental transformation in the nature of the nuclear age. Proponents have also sought to make SDI seem less exotic, less alien, hence less dangerous by comparing it to seemingly benign instruments of defense. Far from being "Star Wars," a science fiction fantasy, strategic defense ideology presented SDI as something well within the common experience of most people.

The president himself was a good source of such domestic images. Upon his return from the Iceland summit, Phyllis Schlafly spoke approvingly of Reagan's ability to convey his belief in SDI. He made it come alive, she said, "with homey analogies that everyone can understand." The president spoke often of SDI as the modern equivalent of a gas mask: even if nuclear weapons were banned, he argued, SDI would function just like a gas mask, as an insurance policy of sorts. While speaking to high school students at Fort McHenry, where American troops withstood a British naval bombardment during the War of 1812, the president compared the "far-sighted" individuals who built the fort to the scientists at work on SDI. This space age defense, he declared, would be "our modern day Ft. McHenry," which would protect people just as the old fort "shielded Baltimore from cannon attack." Caspar Weinberger compared SDI to the "layered defenses of an aircraft carrier battle group," and the *Wall Street Journal*'s Vermont Royster likened it to a bronze shield, providing protection against "spears." Malcolm S. Forbes, Jr., offered an even more benign comparison, assuring *Forbes* readers that, contrary to warnings, SDI was not dangerous but was more like a burglar alarm.[32]

SDI became a powerful symbol of deliverance in the mid-1980s. Fortified by the president's fervor, and with the Grand Vision set before the nation, proponents of missile defense were able to draw upon recognizable cultural traditions as well as public desires generated by nuclear age anxieties. SDI symbolized the popular but often unstated assumption that superpower conflict would inevitably continue in space. "How many Americans," Kevin Phillips asked, "do *not* believe that space is the next battleground, do *not* believe that we, or our children, or their children, will be fighting computerized war out among the planets and distant solar systems? Probably very few."[33] Missile defense would, in this view, replace nuclear weapons as a symbol of protection and salvation from the forces of evil.

The Strategic Defense Initiative also symbolized the belief that Amer-

ica's ultimate destiny—the ability to escape from the horrors of the nuclear age—was at hand. Given the proper mix of political and patriotic will, the steady, inexorable thrust of American technology would bring about the conquest of the final frontier and prepare the way for a restored and transformed nation to reshape its destiny. SDI proponents characterized those who were not so moved by the Vision as "conceptual dinosaurs," stuck forever in the enervating, illusory, and ultimately suicidal world of Mutual Assured Destruction. Due to their failure of nerve and their wish to appease the Soviet Union, opponents of missile defense could not make a commitment to this new path of salvation. Further, they exhibited intellectual dishonesty by cloaking political objections to SDI in the language of science. And so, armed with the fervor of true believers, SDI enthusiasts would go forth, bringing to the American public an ideology that promised a "new way of thinking," doing battle with the formidable forces arrayed against them.

3

Endless Vulnerability: SDI Opponents and the Nature of the Nuclear Age

The shapers of the strategic defense ideology won a clear victory in the battle over visions of utopian futures. Antinuclear activists, like SDI enthusiasts, hoped for a world transformed, not through missile defense, but through the eventual abolition of nuclear weapons. To many people, however, abolition *seemed* more "utopian" than missile defense, largely because the shapers of strategic defense ideology were able to locate missile defense within recognizable and appealing cultural traditions. Antinuclear activists had lost the battle and, given their dislike of SDI, had to make common cause with "establishment doves"—men like Robert McNamara, McGeorge Bundy, George Kennan, and Gerard Smith—whose sense of the fundamental nature of the nuclear age had often been at odds with the antinuclear movement's optimism that dramatic change *was* possible.

Establishment doves continually called attention to what they believed was the primary truth about the nature of the world: mutual vulnerability was, in the words of former Under Secretary of the Navy Townsend Hoopes, "the fundamental existential condition of the age." Gloom and doom had been proclaimed since the dawn of the atomic age. J. Robert Oppenheimer captured the essence of this delicate balance of terror when he said in 1953: "We may anticipate a state of affairs in which the two Great Powers will each be in a position to put an end to the civilization and life of the other, though not without risking its own. We may be likened to two scorpions in a bottle, each capable of killing the other, but only at a risk of his own life."[1]

Established wisdom agreed that even in the 1980s the scorpions were still trapped in Oppenheimer's bottle. Former Secretary of Defense James Schlesinger's comment on the illusory promise of missile defense for the population conveyed this: "There is no serious likelihood of removing the nuclear threat from our cities in our lifetime—or in the lifetime of our children. If these cities are going to be protected, they will be protected either through effective deterrence or through the forebearance of those on the other side."[2]

For those who had been led to the sorrowful realization that the prenuclear age was forever gone, the Grand Vision appeared as a futile and dangerous attempt to avoid facing the political and strategic realities of the age of vulnerability. Consequently, SDI opponents worked with symbols designed to undermine and negate what they understood as the inflated and ultimately dangerous images used to shape strategic defense ideology. It was the gap between these images and what, for opponents, constituted the reality of the situation that bothered those who were contemptuous of the Vision. Accordingly, in May 1986, during an appearance on ABC's "SDI: Windfall or Payoff," the Kennedy School's Joseph Nye remarked that the SDI program needed "about half the money and twice the accuracy in advertising." Part of the task, then, for those opposing SDI was to begin the process of "demystification," to show the American public that uncritical acceptance of the strategic defense ideology would only generate dangerous illusions about the possibilities of missile defense.[3]

Opponents emphasized that President Reagan's Vision did not, in fact, represent a creative response to Einstein's call for a "new way of thinking" engendered by the dangers of the nuclear age. Two prominent opponents, Jack Ruina, director of MIT's Defense and Arms Control Studies Program and former director of DARPA, and MIT's George Rathjens, found it extraordinary that the president would launch a "theoretically laudable, but technically baseless" program that was "irreconcilable with both state-of-the-art technology and . . . nuclear stability." They concluded that SDI stood out as "the most bizarre episode in the sad history of the nuclear arms race."[4] Others attacked the compelling image of SDI as a technologically achievable and morally commendable system that would usher in a more secure world. A few opponents also tried to interest the public in an alternative vision of humankind's potential use of the final frontier of space.

Editorial cartoonist Jeff Danziger of the *Christian Science Monitor* captured the fears of those who worried about the destabilizing effects of SDI with a portrayal of the barbarian of war offering the sword of space weaponry to humankind, with his elbow resting on the book of history. Clearly, Danziger hoped that readers would learn from history that war, not peace, came from qualitative leaps in weapons systems. Ken Alexander saw SDI as the equivalent of Linus's security blanket, and Steve Greenberg of the *Seattle Post Intelligencer* thought of it as a night-light, one of a number of childish comforts for the president but certainly inappropriate as a mature response to the dilemmas of the nuclear age. Other cartoonists dramatized the enduring nature of vulnerability. Tom Kerr of the *Asbury Park Press* and Jim Morin called attention to the inadequacy of any space umbrella in the face of thousands of Soviet missiles. In the *Boston Globe,* Dan Wasserman mocked the ability of SDI to affect "real world" events, while Dick Locher reminded his readers that missile defense could never stop such primitive yet effective forms of warfare as car bombs and dynamite-carrying terrorists.

Some opponents sought to locate the seductive appeal of SDI in what historian Paul Boyer called "dark and deeply rooted" themes in American culture. He and several other cultural analysts perceived SDI as a virulent expression of American self-reliance and innocence, which made missile defense so attractive. According to Boyer, it was the power of these cultural traditions that blinded people to the stark realization that no nation could guarantee its citizens' security in isolation from the rest of the world. Vulnerability and security had to be understood as global issues, and no nation, not even the United States, could take fate into its own hands.[5]

Harsher still was British antinuclear activist E. P. Thompson, who warned that this posture of cultural innocence merely masked what SDI *really* signified: the American desire to return to the "years of

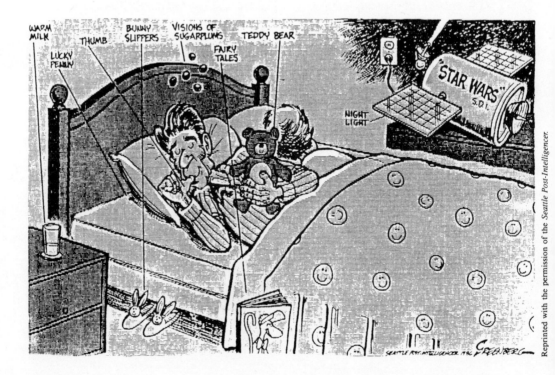

Reprinted with the permission of Thomas F. Kerr and the *Asbury Park Press*.

© 1987, *Boston Globe*. Reprinted by permission.

How Star Wars Works....

(A.) SOVIET UNION FIRES NUCLEAR MISSILES AT U.S. (B.) STAR WARS INTERCEPTS MISSILES AND (C.) DESTROYS THEM. (D.) SOVIETS LAUNCH MORE MISSILES (E.) AND MORE MISSILES (F.) AND MORE MISSILES (G.) AND MORE (H.) AND MORE (I.) AND MORE MISSILES (J.) AND MORE (K.) AND MORE (L.) AND MORE (M.) AND MORE

MODERN WARFARE

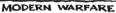

American superiority, 1945-1950." He accused the United States of seeking to wage the cold war in space in order to take advantage of American superiority in high-tech weaponry and declared that the "ideological delirum" of the revitalized cold war in America that gave birth to SDI was "attuned to all the worst traditions of American right-wing populism." Others also saw cold war impulses in the Vision, including the editors of *Christianity and Crisis,* who declared that SDI emerged "not for love of peace, but lust for hegemony." In one of the angriest editorials written about SDI, the *Progressive's* Erwin Knoll called this veiled attempt at superiority the latest in a long line of President Reagan's "contemptible manifestations of official deception." To suggest that space weaponry was the "key to a decent, humane and peaceful future" was, Knoll said, "to tell the biggest lie."[6]

Enemies of missile defense often called attention to the technological hubris that was integral to arguments made in favor of SDI. The loss of the Challenger and the explosion of the nuclear reactor at Chernobyl provided SDI opponents an opportunity to remind the public how dangerous it was to place ultimate confidence in any complex technological system. Even before the searing icon of the Challenger burned itself into the nation's memory, however, editorial comment noted that other, less catastrophic setbacks with shuttle missions did not bode well for SDI. Focusing on a series of problems that forced the postponement of one shuttle mission, the *Boston Globe* wondered, "Will Star Wars Work Perfectly? Ask Cape Canaveral." Nicholas Wade, writing in the *New York Times* in 1985, listed a series of extensive problems in a "successful" Challenger mission and reminded readers that the troubled flight had "no Russians to contend with, only internal design flaws or operational errors."[7]

Opponents also tried to counter the attempt of the president to turn the death of the Challenger astronauts into part of a heroic saga of the conquest of space. James Reston, for example, not only worried about faulty technology but thought the episode called into question whether "the bravery of the pioneers who conquered this continent [was] the 'right stuff' to bring peace on earth or conquer space." Other editorials expressed the belief that the event certainly should prove that faith in SDI was unwarranted. "Would we, as a nation," asked the *Philadelphia Inquirer,* "be willing to stake our very survival on the premise that no errors would ever occur?" The editors of *America,* a Catholic journal, reminded readers that the kind of technological perfection that made SDI so appealing was not possible in a "finite world composed of limited human beings."[8]

Of course, SDI supporters responded that these were the wrong lessons to be learned. The shuttle disaster taught us nothing about SDI, claimed William F. Buckley, for neither the space program nor SDI should ever be challenged as "intrinsically deficient, or even problematic." Likewise, the disaster moved Phyllis Schlafly to ask not about the reliability of American space technology but whether the Russians were "engaged in a worldwide strategy to sabotage our SDI and our space program."[9]

The accident at Chernobyl also engendered reflection on SDI. Both Ellen Goodman of the *Washington Post* and Anthony Lewis of the *New York Times* understood the real lesson to be the inadequacy of human beings to control nuclear energy or nuclear weapons without inevitable disaster. In light of Chernobyl, faith in SDI was, Lewis thought, "close to irrational." Sen. J. Bennett Johnston (D., La.) raised the spectre of "hundreds of Chernobyls . . . in space" as he described a far-fetched plan to use orbiting nuclear-powered generating stations to supply power to laser weapons.[10]

The battle over the proper symbolic interpretation of such events continued, with Schlafly telling readers of her newsletter that if the Soviets could make such a serious human error at Chernobyl, the United States could not "afford . . . to be the victims of a Soviet human error about nuclear missiles." SDI, she said, could "defend us from a military Chernobyl as well as from a deliberate attack."[11] Jim Morin captured the fears of many SDI opponents that the advance technology to be used in missile defense could also be used to wage an aggressive war from space. Jimmy Margulies and Dan Wasserman illustrated the crisis of confidence in American faith in technology that these events brought about, and Calvin Grondahl of the *Deseret News* mocked what he perceived as the president's continued—and mistaken—reliance on cold war imagery to think about space.

SDI opponents also raised questions about the extravagant claims for the social significance of SDI weapons tests. The editors of the *St. Louis Post-Dispatch* were not moved by the excitement over the Homing Overlay Experiment. They derided HOE as "test-bed technology" and argued that it offered "false hope." Similarly, a letter to the editor of the *Wall Street Journal* claimed that a "one-to-one test against a pre-planned and cooperative target bears little relationship to the expected threat."[12]

In addition to the attempts to generate skepticism regarding technological miracles and the image of meaningful progress portrayed in reports about SDI tests, a number of secular and religious opponents took issue with the argument that SDI represented a morally superior response to the nuclear age. Joseph Nye, author of *Nuclear Ethics,* declared that the moral arguments in favor of SDI displayed "stunted

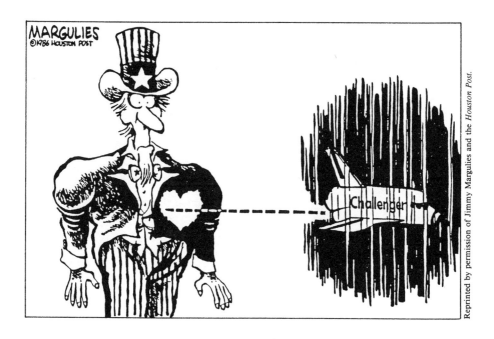

Endless Vulnerability   81

Reprinted by permission of NEA, Inc.

moral reasoning." SDI, he argued, was "no more a moral imperative than were alternative ways of enhancing deterrence." In his view, the morality of the program would "depend on the consequences, not the motives." Representatives of the mainline religious press also criticized the "stunted reasoning" of SDI supporters. David Heim of the *Christian Century* called moral support of SDI "misplaced idealism." MAD was not the best of all possible worlds, he said, but it at least offered a certain "moral symmetry."[13]

A growing number of church groups began to criticize SDI, relying not on a distinctive theological critique of the program but on well-developed secular arguments. By pointing out how SDI endangered stability and the arms control process, many of these groups implicitly endorsed the arguments of the establishment doves: living with some nuclear weapons would be necessary for the foreseeable future. By late 1984 the Unitarian Universalists passed a resolution to "Stop Space Weapons: Resume Space Cooperation," and the general board of the Church of the Brethren offered a resolution to "Keep Outer Space Weapon-Free." In 1985 the Friends Service Committee stated, "We have no faith in Star Wars," and it added that SDI would lead to the "material and spiritual impoverishment of our people." The Reformed Church in America, the Christian Church (Disciples of Christ), the Episcopal Diocese of Washington, D.C., and the United Church of Christ all declared in 1985 that SDI would initiate an arms race in space and lead to a more dangerous world. In 1986 the 198th General Assembly of the Presbyterian Church (U.S.A.) called for a halt to "research, development, and testing plans for space-based missile defense systems."[14]

The United Methodist Council of Bishops finished a two-year study of nuclear issues in 1985 that led to publication of *In Defense of Creation: The Nuclear Crisis and a Just Peace*. The bishops noted "overwhelming skepticism" about SDI among scientists and worried about SDI's offensive implications, its effect upon arms control, and its cost. They found support for their stance in the Bible, reminding readers how often the "Scriptures warn us against false hopes for peace and security." Robert Jewett, professor of New Testament at Garrett Evangelical Seminary, drew a similar lesson. He wrote in *Christian Century* that Isaiah had once warned against a false sense of security when the Israelites signed a mutual defense treaty with Egypt some twenty-seven centuries ago. SDI, he cautioned readers, offered those same "fatal illusions." The editors of *Sojourners* understood the president's Grand Vision speech to be the "first blow of a concerted effort to co-opt the peace movement . . . and steal the moral high ground." They called attention to Peace Pentecost Sunday, June 7, 1987, when churches across the nation planned to protest the "idolatry" of placing "hope for security in technology of our own design."[15]

Some Catholics, including several bishops who were instrumental in shaping "The Challenge of Peace," took issue with the claim that SDI was the only morally appropriate response to their 1983 pastoral letter. In his impassioned argument against SDI, priest and former congressman Robert F. Drinan argued against rushing to alter the nature of deterrence, for "deterrence is the only reason Vatican II and now the U.S. Bishops permit at least on a temporary basis possession of nuclear weapons." The editors of *America* declared that the peace promised by SDI was not the "true peace" envisioned in the bishops' letter, for such a peace could not be realized via a "machine we can buy."[16] Tom Toles, one of the few editorial cartoonists to cleverly mock the moral pretensions of SDI, portrayed the president (Mr. Gazoo) responding to the wise man's question "What is morality?" with the cure-all: SDI.

Joseph Cardinal Bernardin, the archbishop of Chicago, and John Cardinal O'Connor, the archbishop of New York, commented at length about SDI in testimony before the House Foreign Service Committee

in June 1984, during a debate over the MX missile. In their joint written statement they argued that "technological decisions must be governed by political choices which in turn should be governed by a moral vision." Bernardin especially questioned the wisdom of SDI, noting that while its "objectives are desirable," the consequences might not be. The two bishops concluded: "From the perspective of our Pastoral Letter, we support efforts to prevent the initiation of a nuclear race on yet another frontier—outer space." Almost a year later, in a speech prepared for a conference on religion and international relations held at the University of Missouri at Columbia, Bernardin reiterated his "misgivings" about SDI: "While I understand the motivation behind the SDI, I am very skeptical of its consequences on the arms race."[17]

Strategic defense ideology presented SDI as a powerful vision of restoration and transformation, an antidote to the poisonous climate engendered by MAD. Accordingly, some opponents realized that in addition to appealing to the public's skepticism about technology, they needed to present an emotionally appealing vision of the future. Sen. Spark Matsunaga (D., Hawaii) recognized the importance of the symbolic battle when he said, "Star Wars is a vision of our future in space. Only an alternative vision of the future can decisively counter it." An oft-cited text supporting such an alternative vision came from John F. Kennedy: "For the eyes of the world now look into space . . . and we have vowed that we shall not see it governed by a hostile flag of conquest, but by a banner of peace and freedom. We have vowed that we shall not see space filled with weapons of mass destruction, but with instruments of knowledge and understanding."[18]

Matsunaga and others used recollections of past superpower cooperation in space to argue for a nonmilitaristic vision of the human future on the last frontier. Memories of the Apollo-Soyuz mission in 1975 led to grass-roots attempts to bring such an alternative vision into being. During the 1983-84 subcommittee hearing on arms control in outer space, Rep. Mel Levine (D., Calif.) outlined areas of space research where cooperative ventures between the superpowers were already in progress. Also in 1984, Public Law 98-562, "Cooperative East-West Ventures," stated that an "arms race in space . . . [is] in the interests of no one." The law challenged Congress to explore the possibilities of a joint shuttle/Salyut program and a renewal of the Space Cooperation Agreement with the Soviet Union that the United States had failed to renew in 1982. It also called for further superpower cooperation in "space medicine and space biology, planetary science, manned and unmanned space exploration." In the fall of 1984, the Senate conducted hearings on East-West cooperation in outer space, during which Matsunaga expressed optimism that human beings could reach a new stage of development through the proper use of space. SDI, by contrast, was a "perversion of the uniquely human capacity to create great new transcendent forms that unify."[19]

Both science fiction writer Arthur C. Clarke and Carl Sagan argued for a dramatic event that would signal humankind's ability to create "great new transcendent forms that unify." Appearing before Matsunaga's Senate hearing in 1984, Clarke showed a videotape called "A Martian Odyssey" and joined Sagan in proposing a joint U.S.-Soviet manned mission to Mars in 1992. Such a venture would celebrate the 500th anniversary of Columbus landing in the New World and the 75th anniversary of the Russian Revolution. The *St. Louis Post-Dispatch* editorialized that this kind of cooperative venture in space would "fire the world's imagination and . . . lead to a lessening of East-West political tensions." This and other proposals for creative alternatives to SDI—PEACESAT satellites designed to monitor military activities and track arms control compliance, global search-and-rescue operations—prompted Jack Kidd, writing in the *Humanist,* to call for a "Strategic Cooperation Initiative . . . or 'Star Light' strategy."[20]

Cartoonist Jim Borgman of the *Cincinnati Enquirer,* skillfully blending the popular introductory phrase from the movie *Star Wars* with the words of the first American astronauts to land on the moon, awakened memories of superpower cooperation in space, while Jim Morin dramatized the "perversion" brought about by space weapons. Patricia Mische, author of *Star Wars and the State of Our Souls,* also argued that SDI was a "perversion," one that would lead to an impoverished human future. She envisioned human beings having reached the climactic point in their cultural evolution, preparing to occupy the frontier of space, a sacred sanctuary that should not be despoiled by new forms of weaponry. Indeed, the stark choice that faced the superpowers would determine for all humankind whether, in the "sacred journey" into space, "violence will triumph in our psyches and souls . . . or [whether] our indwelling in one another and the earth" would erase the "illusion of our separateness."[21]

In his unsuccessful 1984 presidential campaign, Walter Mondale also argued against SDI on the grounds that it would be the desecration of a sacred realm. He asked, "Why don't we just stop this madness now and draw a line and keep the heavens free from war?"[22] Cartoonists Tony Auth, Don Wright, and Tom Toles all dramatized versions of this desecration of the "heavens."

In their attempts to increase public skepticism about technological miracles and easy answers to the moral dilemmas of the nuclear age,

A LONG TIME AGO, IN AN ADMINISTRATION FAR, FAR AWAY....

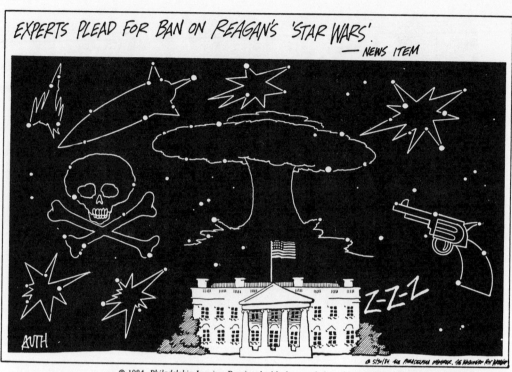

SDI opponents criticized the program from every conceivable angle. Elite discussions focused, for example, on the cost and the vast array of technological questions—from the adequacy of computer programs to the size of rockets needed to lift various components into space—as well as on arms control in general and the ABM treaty in particular. These issues were raised in an explosion of books and articles, in newspaper editorials, and in speeches and debates with proponents of SDI. Yet all of these arguments, no matter how sound, did not do battle with SDI on its own level—that of the emotional satisfaction brought about by image achievement.

Daniel Graham of High Frontier, Inc., had a folksy response to those who argued that SDI would not work: "I just say, 'Fine, you say it won't work. We say it will. Why not give us a chance?' "[23] This recourse to the American sense of fair play, of giving one's opponent a fighting chance, certainly seemed to make sense, especially when it might result in saving people from nuclear destruction. No matter how cogent their arguments, SDI opponents were seen as mere "naysayers," ready to criticize the president's Grand Vision but offering only an unpalatable status quo as an alternative. "Living with nuclear weapons," even in greatly reduced numbers, might be a rational response to the dilemmas of the time, but it could not match SDI as a hopeful response to deeply felt fears.

Only one group of SDI opponents was able to sustain a vibrant battle on the symbolic level: namely, editorial cartoonists critical of the idea of missile defense. Like those SDI enthusiasts who domesticated the Vision, anti-SDI cartoonists used recognizable images from ordinary life to subvert it. While elite discussion could raise questions about the various rationales for missile defense, as well as the strengths and weaknesses of each, Toles, Tom Engelhardt of the *St. Louis Post-Dispatch,* Edward Gamble of the *Florida Times Union,* Dan Wasserman, Borgman, and Steve Greenberg could mock, in a publicly accessible manner, what they saw as the fundamental incoherence of the program. In a similar vein, Tony Auth, Ken Alexander, and Greenberg joined Jerry Fearing of the *St. Paul Pioneer Press-Dispatch* in dramatizing widespread worries that SDI introduced a troublesome new variable into arms control discussions and was especially threatening to the ABM treaty of 1972. Fearing, Linda Boileau, and Chris O'Brion of the *Chapel Hill Newspaper* also commented on the related fear that the contentious issue of SDI would wreck the 1986 Reykjavík summit.

While few people had the necessary time, inclination, or expertise to decipher arguments about the economic cost of SDI, cartoonists Jimmy Margulies, Brian Barling, Paul Conrad, Cahn Lowe of the *Ft. Lauderdale News/Sentinel,* Greenberg, and Borgman dramatized the economic cost using familiar images. Margulies also cleverly declared his lack of confidence in the quality of the SDI "merchandise" that all these millions of dollars were buying, while Alexander, Joel Pett, Chip Bok of the *Akron Beacon Journal,* and Bill Plympton added their voices to those who decried the social cost of SDI.

Both elite and popular criticisms of SDI were designed to convince the public that the marketing campaign in favor of SDI—the attempt to domesticate Reagan's Grand Vision—was fundamentally dishonest. Opponents declared that SDI *did* belong in the realm of science fiction fancy, that it was a dangerously exotic idea and deserved to be treated as such. Furthermore, argued opponents, the comforting images used by SDI enthusiasts to help people "understand" what SDI was about only contributed to the mystification of the Vision.

92   *Symbolic Defense*

© 1986, Tom Engelhardt in the *St. Louis Post-Dispatch*. Reprinted with permission.

'In Hollywood, We Revised Scripts All The Time'

© 1985, Florida Times-Union.

© 1985, Boston Globe. Reprinted by permission.

Endless Vulnerability 95

Reprinted with the permission of the *Seattle Post-Intelligencer.*

Reprinted with the permission of Ken Alexander.

Endless Vulnerability   97

Reprinted with the permission of Jerome W. Fearing and the *St. Paul Pioneer Press-Dispatch.*

Reprinted with the permission of Jerome W. Fearing and the *St. Paul Pioneer Press-Dispatch.*

Reprinted with the permission of Jerome W. Fearing and the *St. Paul Pioneer Press-Dispatch.*

Linda Boileau, *Frankfort State Journal*—ROTHCO.

Reprinted with the permission of Chris O'Brion and the *Chapel Hill Newspaper.*

Endless Vulnerability   99

Reprinted with the permission of Jimmy Margulies and the *Houston Post*.

Barling in the *Christian Science Monitor*; © 1984, TCSPS.

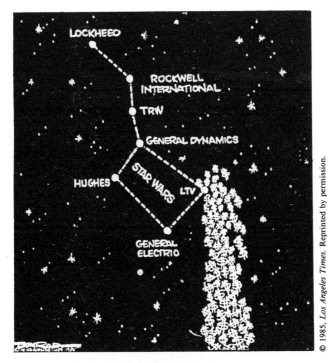

THE BIG DIPPER

If you think Air Force toilet seats are expensive . . . .

Reprinted by permission: Tribune Media Services.

Reprinted with the permission of the *Seattle Post-Intelligencer.*

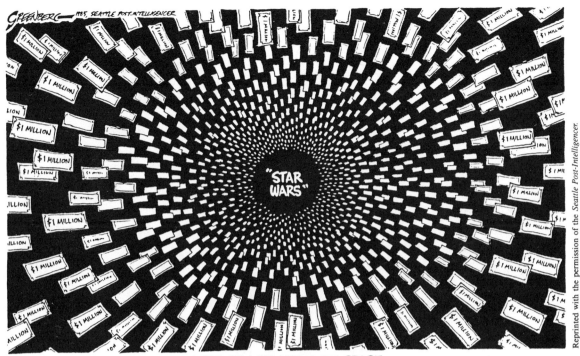

THE BLACK HOLE OF SPACE

" Uh, Congressman, I'll ask you please not to kick the tires anymore..."

Reprinted with the permission of Craig MacIntosh and the *Minneapolis Star-Tribune.*

It was inevitable, perhaps, that the battle over the proper symbolic interpretation of SDI would eventually move to television. Some supporters were quite enthusiastic about such visual depictions of what a missile defense system might do. Commenting on NBC's September 1984 presentation "The Real Star Wars: Defense in Space," High Frontier, Inc., approved of the "beautiful graphic detail" that explained how a "three-layered satellite system would work today and how future technologies . . . could eventually be added into the system." Countless newspapers and magazines used images like Craig MacIntosh's drawing in the *Minneapolis Star and Tribune* to illustrate how hostile missiles would be shot down with laser weapons, while Flora Lewis of the *New York Times* worried about the subliminal messages such depictions sent. There were not, she noted, "any pictures of defenses that don't exist." The message being sent was that "since people can make the designs . . . they can build the things."[24]

Other SDI opponents were bothered by the widespread display of effective defenses. The Union of Concerned Scientists fought back with a television commercial that debuted on May 30, 1985, in Washington, D.C. "Twinkle, Twinkle" showed a little boy dressed in his pajamas holding a teddy bear, sitting by his bedroom window, looking at a night sky bright with stars. As he softly sang "Twinkle, Twinkle, Little Star," one star grew brighter and larger, then finally blew up in his face. After the explosion, the voice of Darth Vader, villain of the *Star Wars* movie, declared, "Stop Star Wars, stop weapons in space."

Several months later, the Coalition for the Strategic Defense Initiative released a television commercial called "Peace Shield," which appeared in fifty cities around the nation. Known to its detractors as the "Crayola ad," it was designed to respond to the UCS's message as well as to build support for SDI in light of the upcoming summit meeting in Iceland. Viewers saw a child's crayon drawing of a family standing outside a little house and heard a young girl say: "I asked my daddy what this 'Star Wars' stuff is all about. He said right now we can't protect ourselves from nuclear weapons, and that's why the president wants to build a peace shield. It'd stop missiles in outer space . . . so they couldn't hit our house. Then nobody could win a war, and if nobody could win a war, there's no reason to start one. My daddy's smart." As the child talked in such human terms about strategic vulnerability, the facial expression of the sun turned sad, but as she spoke of the promise of a peace shield, a protective dome magically appeared over the family and their house, enemy missiles bounced harmlessly off the dome, the sun smiled, and the American flag flew overhead.[25]

In the never-ending battle to make doubts about SDI as persuasive as hopes, several takeoffs on the "Peace Shield" commercial appeared. In Art Buchwald's commentary, a little girl drew a protective umbrella over the earth while her mother told a skeptical father, "If kids believe a blue crayon can stop a red one they won't be afraid." The father took a black crayon, sliced through the shield, and told his little girl, "Don't believe everything you see on television."[26] Herblock, Jimmy Margulies, Garry Trudeau, and Tom Toles also took aim at the "Peace Shield" in their cartoons.

From *Herblock at Large* (New York: Pantheon Books, 1987).

Reprinted with the permission of Jimmy Margulies and the *Houston Post*.

Doonesbury

A television response, "Space Wars I," was released by the Committee for a Strong and Peaceful America, a coalition of eight arms control groups. According to Ann Cahn, "Space Wars I" was an attempt to "expose the deceptive message in the 'Crayola' commercial that Star Wars will 'shield' or protect Americans during a nuclear attack." In "Space Wars I," a little boy watched the beginning of the "Peace Shield" commercial on television while playing with lettered blocks. A narrator said: "Matthew has the same problem the White House does. He's trying to turn Star Wars into something called the Peace Shield. But it doesn't fit. Because Matthew's learning what adults already know. When someone wants to mislead you, then they try to change the name. But when you look closer, it's still the same old thing." At this point, Matthew shouted, "I've got it," and assembled his blocks to convey the message "Space Wars!"[27]

George Lucas, the creator of the *Star Wars* trilogy, was distressed that various advocacy groups were using his movie name to describe missile defense, and he brought suit against High Frontier, Inc., and the Committee for a Strong and Peaceful America. His lawyer, Laurence Hefter, argued that because the commercials associated the name with missile defense, children would be "turned off by [them] . . . and would shy away from the movie and its spin-off products, such as dolls, toys, comic books, cookies, paper cups, watches, candles and bubble bath." However, U.S. District Court Judge Gerhard Gesell ruled that anyone could use the term "Star Wars" in "parody or descriptively to further a communication of their views on S.D.I."[28]

While all of these commercials appeared on selected national markets for only short periods of time, they received far greater exposure since network news programs and *Time* magazine ran stories on the "battle" of SDI television advertisements. On the November 14, 1985, edition of "CBS Evening News," for example, Henry Kendall of the Union of Concerned Scientists and Daniel Graham discussed the virtues of their respective spots. Kendall thought the "Crayola ad" a "fraud on the American public," to which Graham responded, "Our child gets protected. . . . in the Union of Concerned Scientists [ad], she [*sic*] gets blown up."[29]

SDI opponents used symbols of negation and subversion to attack what they considered to be the seductive power of the strategic defense ideology. All of their objections stemmed from the uncomfortable truth that nuclear vulnerability was as much a part of reality as the air people breathed. They portrayed SDI as technologically defective, dangerous to the state of nuclear stability between the superpowers, horrendously expensive, and a morally flawed response to the perils of the nuclear age. Like conservative critics of world government or complete nuclear disarmament, SDI opponents asked Americans to avoid the temptation of utopian visions that promised salvation through missile defense.

Conclusion: The Enduring Appeal of the Grand Vision

SDI emerged out of the third period of American cultural anxiety regarding nuclear weapons and nuclear war. The nuclear fears of each of the first two periods, 1945-50 and 1954-63, came about because of real-world events: the awesome power of the atomic bomb evident in the destruction of Hiroshima and Nagasaki, and the ensuing cold war with the Soviet Union. Both engendered the gnawing fear that the United States would someday feel the horror of atomic attack, which in turn propelled concerned Americans to call for world government or for more nuclear weapons as the ultimate safeguard of our security.

During the mid-1950s, nuclear fears were aroused by the widely publicized danger of radioactive fallout from atmospheric nuclear testing. Also, the Berlin crisis, which began in 1958, brought to American television the spectre of Soviet and American tanks facing each other only a few yards apart at Checkpoint Charlie. Berlin would remain a chronic concern until after the resolution of the Cuban missile crisis of 1962. The latter, of course, still symbolizes to many Americans the most dangerous few days in the history of the nuclear age: when the superpowers went to the brink and stepped back. After the peaceful resolution of the Berlin and Cuban crises, and the signing of the Limited Test Ban Treaty in 1963, intense nuclear anxieties did not resurface until the "great awakening" of the late 1970s. The new crisis mentality differed, however, in one significant respect: namely, there was no major international crisis that prompted it, nothing remotely approaching the danger of the Berlin or Cuban episodes.

Certainly, the Committee on the Present Danger must be given credit for skillfully manipulating the recognizable contours of the cold war worldview in order to raise the spectre of an America endangered by a Window of Vulnerability. Coming at a time when Americans felt victimized — as by the holding of hostages in Iran and the Soviet Union's invasion of Afghanistan, which led to a breakdown of the arms control process — ultimate victimization from a nuclear attack *seemed* more plausible than it might have several years earlier. Ironically, as the

committee sounded the clarion call for Americans to rouse their martial sensibilities, it also sparked fears that nuclear war was close at hand.

Several members of the Reagan administration fueled those fears with ill-chosen words about the possibility of fighting and winning limited nuclear wars. This made it easier for the antinuclear movement to convince a significant number of people that nuclear danger resulted from the very existence of large numbers of nuclear weapons, not from specific conflict situations. Hence, popular wisdom declared that nuclear danger was constantly high; it existed at the same level at all times, and no one would be safe until nuclear weapons were no more. The cold war rhetoric, and spirited challenges to that rhetoric, thus created a sense of crisis in a period when there was no crisis.

Nevertheless, in such an emotionally charged atmosphere, it came as no surprise that both antinuclear activists and missile defense enthusiasts were attracted to images of radical transformation of the world, presented as symbols of hope but certainly emerging out of deep despair. As détente and arms control, the pillars of superpower stability, crumbled, feelings of vulnerability increased and visions of radical change became attractive.

Such responses could be fought on a purely symbolic battleground within the culture because there was no real-world crisis that demanded concrete action. Consequently, adherents of the Nuclear Freeze could devote their energies to the symbolic politics of passage of a freeze resolution in national and state legislative bodies, while more strident antinuclear activists could envision themselves as the latest in a long line of social reformers, devoted to the immediate and complete abolition of nuclear weapons. Starting from a different place on the ideological spectrum, SDI enthusiasts could blend cold war fears of the Soviet Union, widespread ambivalence toward deterrence, and a deeply felt need for a new path to peace into an appealing vision of missile defense.

Strategic defense ideology offered the American public more than just rational arguments for the virtues of missile defense. It provided as well the outlines of a new public philosophy regarding the nature and meaning of the nuclear age. Americans were asked to respond to nuclear danger as patriots, to draw on the intuitive genius of American know-how to build a "thing" that would make the nation safe. The ideology drew freely from orthodox cold war mentalities and from antinuclear critiques of deterrence, popular exhortations about the horrors of nuclear war, and the perceived need for radical change in an intolerable nuclear status quo. Its goal was to eliminate weapons, not people, an explicit prolife message for the nuclear age.

Those who opposed the strategic defense ideology had to respond to visionary innovation with the warning that it would be well to respect the traditional wisdom of the nuclear age. The message was one of little comfort: living with nuclear weapons was part of the human condition, although we could, perhaps, choose to live with fewer weapons. Above all, visions of abolition *or* protection were illusory. Modest but useful innovation in crisis prevention and crisis control and modest but useful progress in arms control were the keys to a stable future. Managerial stoicism, rather than utopian enthusiasm, was the appropriate response to nuclear danger. SDI opponents reminded people of past arms races that had been celebrated as ways to make the world more secure but had, in fact, made the world more dangerous. They also sought to awaken the sense of technological skepticism that, paradoxically, often accompanied uncritical confidence in technological achievement.

The battle between strategic defense ideology and the traditional wisdom of the nuclear age was a partisan one. Missile defense became a highly charged issue, not only because it was a powerful symbol in itself, but because people, in responding in a variety of ways to SDI, often found themselves involved in the creative work of reconstructing their whole sense of the contours and the meaning of the nuclear age. It was as if SDI had forced a reexamination of post-1945 first principles, and as individuals responded to this challenge, they sought to locate themselves within the recognizable symbolic landscape of American cultural traditions.

The battle over the proper definition of nuclear age first principles was most graphically evident in my visits with fervent SDI supporters and opponents in Washington, D.C. It was a jarring experience. In the few minutes it took to walk from the Heritage Foundation or High Frontier, Inc., to the Arms Control Association or the Center for Defense Information, I left and entered two very different worlds. People could not even agree on the fundamental nature of the nuclear age, let alone what missile defense might mean. Surely, it is this profound argument regarding the nature of the nuclear world, and America's proper role in that world, that is at the heart of the debates about SDI.

Both supporters and opponents of missile defense used the rich symbolic resources available to them in order to convert people to their view of things. In this regard, editorial cartoonists, through their clever manipulation of popular images, played an important role in the generation of symbols that constituted the weapons used in the ongoing cultural battle. Some of their cartoons reflected the urge to enshrine certain first principles about the nature of the nuclear world. Draper Hill's depiction of the nuclear genie looking contemptuously upon President Reagan's attempt to tame the nuclear age offered a particular statement of faith about the nature of this age and the ability of humankind to substantially alter it. Other cartoonists dramatized the "truth" of endless vulnerability by reminding their readers of the ease with which a guerrilla could plant a bomb or how thousands of Soviet missiles could make the umbrella of missile defense nothing more than a pathetic and futile attempt at security. A quite different assumption was expressed in Alexander Hunter's drawing of an American eagle catching enemy missiles in outer space. The eagle symbolized the animating power of American patriotic will, and the message was clear: through adherence to the strategic defense ideology, Americans *could,* if motivated by the pioneer spirit of the nation's ancestors, take fate into their own hands and escape from the rabid condition in which the liberal doctrine of MAD had placed the world.

Several cartoons dramatized the moral outcome of one's choice of first principles. Jeff Danziger's barbarian of war promised that space weapons brought war, not peace. Conversely, Mike Shelton's "Soviet Star Peace" showed the choice to be made between SDI and enslavement in a global Soviet gulag. Other cartoonists sought to find the proper frame of reference for SDI, domesticating the Grand Vision by proposing various metaphors or analogies. Opponents, for example, compared SDI to science fiction movies or fairy tales, complete with a space fairy, or perceived SDI as a species of twentieth-century infantilism; it was also called "garbage," "hot air," and "witches brew," and comparisons were made to expensive boondoggles such as the infamous high-priced military toilet seat.

Editorial cartoonists sympathetic with SDI worked with very different images. Enthusiasts connected global defense in the nuclear age with the shield, an instrument of defense in conventional wars of the Middle Ages. Images of cold war enemies, particularly the Soviets, were used to make the case for the necessity of missile defense. They were perceived as ravenous and deceitful bears, bullies, or subway toughs; internal enemies were wind-up puppets, "useful idiots" taken in by Soviet propaganda about the desirability of peaceful ventures in space. The great majority of SDI cartoons done by opponents utilized a variety of symbols to ridicule the image achievements of the strategic defense ideology. Anti-SDI cartoonists subjected the president to withering ridicule, as if an attack upon the father of the Grand Vision could render the subject of missile defense unworthy of serious conversation. The images were striking: the president was an eccentric technological tinkerer, dreaming up SDI in bizarre situations; he was a technological infant; he was a doddering old man, happily wandering through space fantasies and childhood fairy tales, blurring fact and fiction in dangerous ways; he was a naked emperor; and he was Darth Vader, the powerful villain of the *Star Wars* movies, who had endangered humankind by conjuring up the "dark side of the force" (SDI) from his cold war mentality.

Pro-SDI cartoonists focused only occasionally on the president, usually as an innocent victim of the evil machinations of the aforementioned Soviet bears and thugs. Reagan appeared as an industrious blacksmith forging a shield for America; as a mild-mannered subway rider wearing a bullet-proof vest; or as a bespectacled student of SDI research, who obviously meant to provoke no one but succeeded in provoking the Soviet bully.

Cartoonists on both sides mocked the scientific integrity of the opposition. Pro-SDI scientists were portrayed as money-hungry, opportunistic, and dishonest, while anti-SDI scientists and their followers were accused of letting ideology shape scientific research. Anti-SDI cartoonists tried to undermine faith in technology by both humorous and serious images of technical fallibility. In a clever display of the use of irony, several cartoonists also dramatized what they believed would be the unpalatable social costs of such an expensive vision.

Anti-SDI cartoonists sought to engender both awe and reverence for "the heavens" and looked nostalgically to the "Golden Age" of superpower cooperation in space, hoping, no doubt, to spark memories of the harmonious images of space in the popular movie *2010* rather than the centuries of war at the heart of the *Star Wars* trilogy. Cartoonists who supported SDI reminded people of the seemingly endless war between the Soviet Union and the United States and argued that the future of the world depended not on the harmonious use of space but on American victory in the race for space supremacy.

What is the significance of reconstructing the cultural life of SDI? What, to use Mircea Eliade's words, does it reveal about our dissatisfactions, drives, and nostalgias? Arising in a period of intense cultural engagement with nuclear fear, SDI appealed to a fundamental nostalgia—the desire to escape from the nuclear age—and, more than any postwar vision of a world transformed through nuclear disarmament, it offered a world "disarmed" through the technological genius of the United States. Whatever the immediate political future of SDI, the development of the strategic defense ideology provided, for the first time, the framework for a conservative political stance that looked to the viability of a transformative vision as the key to life in the nuclear age. The *idea* of missile defense was rooted in a political community noted for single-minded devotion to sacred causes.

The continuing appeal of symbols of deliverance, most notably SDI, reveals not only the seductive power of such symbols but an understandable despair over the failure of the "status quo gang" to "think radically." The appeal of SDI may signify that the long period of uneasy acceptance of mutual vulnerability is coming to an end. Yet, if this condition is, indeed, the "fundamental existential condition of the age," symbols of deliverance like SDI will continue to arise, to enlist popular support, and to perhaps hinder the search for more modest and accessible paths to real security in the continuing age of vulnerability.

Notes

PREFACE

1. Mircea Eliade, *Occultism, Witchcraft, and Cultural Fashions: Essays in Comparative Religion* (Chicago: University of Chicago Press, 1976), 3.

2. Randall Forsberg, "Call to Halt the Nuclear Arms Race: Proposal for a Mutual U.S.-Soviet Nuclear-Weapon Freeze," reprinted in Donna Gregory, *The Nuclear Predicament: A Sourcebook* (New York: St. Martin's Press, 1986), 259-65.

3. A good collection of essays that examines the impact of Nuclear Winter is Lester Grinspoon, ed., *The Long Darkness: Psychological and Moral Perspectives on Nuclear Winter* (New Haven: Yale University Press, 1986). Recently, the inevitability of Nuclear Winter has come under attack. For a good summation of criticism of this symbol, see Russell Seitz, " 'Nuclear Winter' Melts Down," *The National Interest,* no. 5 (Fall 1986): 3-17. Lifton's comments on Nuclear Winter are found in Robert Jay Lifton, *The Future of Immortality and Other Essays for a Nuclear Age* (New York: Basic Books, 1987), 112-14.

4. The testimonies of Carl Sagan and Richard Perle are found in U.S. Congress, House, Committee on Science and Technology and Committee on Interior and Insular Affairs, *Nuclear Winter: Hearings before a Subcommittee of the House Committee on Science and Technology and a Subcommittee of the Committee on Interior and Insular Affairs,* 99th Cong., 1st sess., 1985, pp. 19-68.

5. Flora Lewis, "Freeze That Blarney," *New York Times,* July 8, 1984, p. E21.

INTRODUCTION

1. The best treatment of this theme in the public culture of the time is Paul Boyer's "First Reactions," in Boyer, *By the Bomb's Early Light: American Thought and Culture at the Dawn of the Atomic Age* (New York: Pantheon, 1986), 3-26.

2. Philip Morrison, "If the Bomb Gets Out of Hand," in Dexter Masters and Katharine Way, eds., *One World or None: A Report to the Public on the Full Meaning of the Atomic Bomb* (New York: McGraw-Hill Book Co., 1946), 6; Louis N. Ridenour, "There Is No Defense," in ibid.; Bernard Brodie, *The Absolute Weapon: Atomic Power and World Order* (New York: Harcourt, Brace & Co., 1946), 28.

3. William Higinbotham, "The Road to Security," *Bulletin of the Atomic Scientists* 2, nos. 3 & 4 (Aug. 1, 1946): 27; "President Truman's Speech at

Fordham," ibid. 1, no. 11 (May 15, 1946): 6. See also H. C. Urey, "A Scientist Views the World Situation," ibid. 1, no. 5 (Feb. 15, 1946): 4; Robert M. Hutchins, "Peace or War with Russia?," ibid. 1, no. 6 (Mar. 1, 1946): 2.

4. Sylvia Eberhart, "How the American People Feel about the Atomic Bomb," ibid. 3, nos. 4 & 5 (Apr.-May 1947): 146-49ff.; J. Robert Oppenheimer, "Atomic Weapons and American Policy," ibid. 9, no. 6 (July 1953): 202-5.

5. Roland Sawyer, "It's Up to You, Mr. President," ibid. 9, no. 7 (Sept. 1953): 245-46.

6. Quoted in William F. Vandercook, "The Vision of the 'Prepared' Society," ms. (author's files). The author wishes to thank Mr. Vandercook for permission to draw material from his paper.

7. Most of vol. 9, no. 7 (Sept. 1953) of the *Bulletin of the Atomic Scientists* is devoted to the report of Project East River. On the dispersal of cities, see Tracy B. Augur, "The Dispersal of Cities as a Defense Measure," ibid. 4, no. 3 (Mar. 1948): 131-34; Eugene Rabinowitch, "The Only Real Defense," ibid. 7, no. 9 (Sept. 1951): 241-42. A good bibliography on the concept of dispersal can be found in Berthold Altmann and Harry Moskowitz, comps., "Dispersal: A Selected Bibliography," ibid., 280-84.

8. McElroy's comment is from Richard J. Barber Associates, *The Advanced Research Projects Agency, 1958-1974* (unpublished report, Dec. 1975), I-7. Jack Ruina graciously allowed me to read this manuscript, with its good histories of American attempts at air and missile defense. The ARPA later became the Defense Advanced Research Projects Agency (DARPA).

9. Edward Teller, *The Legacy of Hiroshima* (Garden City, N.Y.: Doubleday & Company, 1962), 128-29. LeMay's comments are found in William J. Broad, " 'Star Wars' Traced to Eisenhower Era," *New York Times,* Oct. 28, 1986, pp. C1, C3. See also Alexander Flax, "Ballistic Missile Defense: Concepts and History," in *Weapons in Space,* vol. 1: *Concepts and Technologies* (*Daedalus* 114, no. 2 [Spring 1985]), 33-52; Jack H. Nunn, *American Air Defense Developments* (Cambridge: Center for International Studies, MIT, Aug. 1980); David N. Schwartz, "Past and Present: The Historical Legacy," in Ashton B. Carter and David B. Schwartz, eds., *Ballistic Missile Defense* (Washington, D.C.: Brookings Institution, 1984), 330-49; Paul Stares, *The Militarization of Space: U.S. Policy 1945-1984* (Ithaca: Cornell University Press, 1985) and *Space Weapons and U.S. Strategy: Origins and Development* (London and Sydney: Croom Helm, 1985).

10. The literature on the history of the great ABM debate of the 1960s and early 1970s is extensive. The best account is Edward Randolph Jayne III, "The ABM Debate: Strategic Defense and National Security" (Ph.D. diss., Dept. of Political Science, MIT, June 1969). A good short history is George Rathjens, "The ABM Debate," in Bernard Brodie, Michael D. Intriligator, and Roman Kolkowicz, eds., *National Security and International Stability* (Cambridge, Mass.: Oelgeschlager, Gunn & Hain, 1983), 379-406. For voices representing both sides of the debate, see American Security Council, *USSR vs. USA: The ABM Debate and the Changed Strategic Balance* (Washington, D.C.: Acropolis Books, 1969); Center for the Study of Democratic Institutions, *Anti-Ballistic Missile: Yes or No?* (New York: Hill and Wang, 1968); Ann Hessing Cahn, "Scientists and the ABM" (Ph.D diss., Dept. of Political Science, MIT, July 1971); Johan J. Holst and William Schneider, Jr., *Why ABM? Policy*

Issues in the Missile Defense Controversy (New York: Pergamon Press, 1969). Periodical literature is also extensive. Some of the most significant articles include: "The Case for Missile Defense," *Foreign Affairs* 43, no. 3 (Apr. 1969): 433-48; Richard L. Garwin and Hans A. Bethe, "Anti-Ballistic Missile Systems," *Scientific American* 218, no. 3 (Mar. 1968): 21-31; George W. Rathjens, "The Dynamics of the Arms Race," ibid. 220, no. 4 (Apr. 1969): 15-25; Jerome B. Wiesner, "The Case against an Anti-Ballistic Missile System," *Look* 31, no. 24 (Nov. 28, 1967): 17-25.

11. Calvin Trillin, "U.S. Journal: Lake County, Ill., Targets," *The New Yorker* (Feb. 15, 1969): 101. Secretary of Defense Robert McNamara's speech on September 18, 1967, in San Francisco describing the dangers of ABM and then outlining a justification for the program can be found in Robert McNamara, *The Essence of Security* (New York: Harper and Row, 1968), chap. 4 and appendix 1.

12. This information is from Cahn, "Scientists and the ABM." In his study of polling information on the American public response to missile defense since 1945, Thomas W. Graham says that a plurality of the public supported ABM through 1970, turning against it only in January 1971 "in the context of opposition to spending additional money for the defense system." See Graham, *Public Attitudes towards Active Defense: ABM and Star Wars, 1945-1985* (Cambridge: Center for International Studies, MIT, 1986), I-4. For a summary of this research, see Thomas W. Graham and Bernard M. Kramer, "The Polls: ABM and Star Wars: Attitudes toward Nuclear Defense, 1945-1985," *Public Opinion Quarterly* 50, no. 1 (Spring 1986): 125-34.

13. David Hoffman, "Reagan Seized Idea Shelved in '80 Race," *Washington Post,* Mar. 3, 1985, p. A19; Robert Scheer, *With Enough Shovels: Reagan, Bush, and Nuclear War* (New York: Random House, 1982), 233.

14. The Center for Defense Information in Washington, D.C., owns a copy of *Murder in the Air,* which I was not permitted to view. I was, however, able to see a copy of part of the script, from which these quotes are taken. The film is also owned by the Turner Entertainment film library, which can be contacted at 213-558-7520. Both Michael Paul Rogin, in *Ronald Reagan, the Movie: And Other Episodes in Political Demonology* (Berkeley: University of California Press, 1987), and Leslie Gelb, in "The Mind of the President," *New York Times Magazine* (Oct. 6, 1985): 21-24ff., point out how important various movie roles have been for the president. Rogin suggests that the role of Brass Bancroft might have been significant in Reagan's enthusiasm for SDI.

15. Edward Teller, "Planning for Peace," *Orbis* (Summer 1966): 341. Reagan's visit to Lawrence Livermore is described in Teller, "SDI: The Last, Best, Hope," *Insight* (Oct. 28, 1985): 75-79.

16. Anderson's comments are in Tina Rosenberg, "The Authorized Version," *Atlantic* (Feb. 1986): 26. See also "1980 Republican National Convention Platform," p. 32 (copy in author's files).

17. Daniel O. Graham, "Proposed Statement of U.S. Policy," in Graham, *High Frontier: A New National Strategy* (Washington, D.C.: Heritage Foundation, 1982), 14. See also George Lardner, Jr., "Gen. Graham's Star Wars," *Washington Post Magazine* (Nov. 17, 1985), p. 14.

18. Quoted in "Max Hunter: The Force behind Reagan's Star Wars Strategy," *Business Week* (June 20, 1983): 56.

19. Watkins's remarks are reported in Hoffman, "Reagan Seized Idea," pp. A1, A19. Reagan's comments are in "Strategic Defense Initiative, with Morton Kondracke and Richard H. Smith of *Newsweek* on 3-4-85," *Weekly Compilation of Presidential Documents* 21, no. 11 (Mar. 18, 1985): 277. General Vessey has a slightly different recollection of the Joint Chiefs' response: "Our recommendation was that we move out into the defensive in the long run." See Frank Greve, "Out of the Blue: How 'Star Wars' Was Proposed," *Philadelphia Inquirer,* Nov. 17, 1985, p. 24A. There are a number of good accounts of the various approaches to missile defense that made an impact on the president. See, for example, Sidney Blumenthal, *The Rise of the Counter-Establishment: From Conservative Ideology to Political Power* (New York: Times Books, 1986), 305-10; William J. Broad, *Star Warriors* (New York: Simon and Schuster, 1985) and "Reagan's 'Star Wars' Bid: Many Ideas Converging," *New York Times,* Mar. 4, 1985; Gregg Herken, "The Earthly Origins of Star Wars," *Bulletin of the Atomic Scientists* 43, no. 8 (Oct. 1987): 20-28; Robert Scheer, "Teller's Obsession Became Reality in 'Star Wars' Plan," *Los Angeles Times,* July 10, 1983, sec. 6, pp. 6-9. Perhaps the most thorough discussion of the origins of SDI is found in Philip M. Boffey, William J. Broad, Leslie H. Gelb, Charles Mohr, and Holcomb B. Noble, *Claiming the Heavens: The* New York Times *Complete Guide to the Star Wars Debate* (New York: Times Books, 1988), 3-25.

20. Nixon is quoted in Strobe Talbott, "The Case against Star Wars Weapons," *Time* (May 7, 1984): 82. For a transcript of President Reagan's "Second American Revolution" speech, see *New York Times,* Feb. 7, 1985, p. B8.

21. Polls taken shortly after the president's speech revealed that the American public was confident such defenses could be built, but it was worried about the cost and about a new arms race in space. Nevertheless, a significant number of those polled thought that missile defense would add to the nation's security. See Graham, *Public Attitudes.* Current (1986-88) public opinion polls reveal that there is more enthusiasm for research than for "building" SDI, that "support for SDI has declined about 10 percentage points [64 to 54] from . . . late 1986, immediately after the Reykjavik summit." Further, one-third of those polled are "firm" opponents and one-quarter are "firm" supporters. Finally, and not surprisingly, attitudes toward SDI are "closely linked to attitudes toward President Reagan." See U.S. Department of State, "An Overview of Current Attitudes toward SDI," information memorandum, Dec. 23, 1987 (author's files).

22. The "Star Wars" section of this address has been reprinted in many places. There are several collections that include the speech and add commentary on the technical, strategic, and moral issues it raised. See, for example, Zbigniew Brzezinski, ed., *Promise or Peril: The Strategic Defense Initiative* (Washington, D.C.: Ethics and Public Policy Center, 1986); Sidney D. Drell, Philip J. Farley, and David Holloway, *The Reagan Strategic Defense Initiative: A Technical, Political, and Arms Control Assessment* (Cambridge, Mass.: Ballinger, 1985); P. Edward Haley and Jack Merritt, *Strategic Defense Initiative: Folly or Future?* (Boulder, Colo.: Westview Press, 1986). The most valuable collection is *Weapons in Space,* vol. 1: *Concepts and Technologies* (*Daedalus* 114, no. 2 [Spring 1985]) and vol. 2: *Implications for Security* (*Daedalus* 114, no. 3 [Summer 1985]). For a helpful analysis of the speech, see Janice Hocker

Rushing, "Ronald Reagan's 'Star Wars' Address: Mythic Containment of Technical Reasoning," *Quarterly Journal of Speech* 72 (1986): 415-33.

23. George W. Ball, "The War for Star Wars," *New York Review of Books* (Apr. 11, 1985): 41.

CHAPTER 1

1. "CBS News Special Report: A Presidential Address" (Mar. 23, 1983), vol. 9, no. 8, p. 8 (transcript on microfilm, Widener Library).

2. Keyworth is quoted in Gregg Herken, "The Earthly Origins of Star Wars," *Bulletin of the Atomic Scientists* 43, no. 8 (Oct. 1987): 25-26. His later comment is in his foreword to Alan Chalfont, *Star Wars: Suicide or Survival?* (London: Weidenfeld and Nicolson, 1985), 7. Like so many supporters of SDI, Keyworth was not consistent in his enthusiasm for or his understanding of the significance of the program. In his 1984 testimony before the Senate Foreign Relations Committee, for example, he said that "none of us has ever proposed, nor do I think any of us believe that we are describing or discussing here some magical shield under which we can live with no concerns. We are talking about an element of our defense posture and a gradual change in strategy... in which the Strategic Defense Initiative will be one single component." Quoted in Larry Pressler, *Star Wars: The Strategic Defense Initiative Debates in Congress* (New York: Praeger, 1986), 123. For the Teller quote, see Edward Teller, "Reagan's Courage," *New York Times,* Mar. 30, 1983, p. A31.

3. "Star Wars Reality," *Wall Street Journal,* Mar. 25, 1983, p. 22; Pete Wilson, " 'Star Wars' Defense beats MAD Alternative," *Los Angeles Times,* Mar. 2, 1984, sec. 2, p. 5; Walter McDougall, "How Not to Think about Space Weapons," *National Review* (May 13, 1983): 554.

4. *High Frontier Newsletter* 1, no. 6 (Nov. 1983): 5. In this same issue, *The Day After* was called an "appeasement" movie. For those troubled by such graphic depictions of nuclear horror, science fiction writer and High Frontier supporter Robert Heinlein offered the comforting belief that missile defense would "save the lives of American citizens... citizens of Western Europe... the Third World, and of Russians themselves by quenching out nuclear war, even after the button is pushed."

5. William Safire, "Farewell to Dempsey," *New York Times,* Mar. 31, 1983, p. A23; "Arms and Mr. Reagan," *Detroit News,* Mar. 25, 1983, p. 8A; Meg Greenfield, "Calling Buck Rogers," *Newsweek* (Apr. 4, 1983): 88. The cover story of this issue of *Newsweek* focused on missile defense, yet the front cover misleadingly asked, "Will Space Be the Next Battleground?"

6. Rathjens is quoted in "CBS News Special Report: The President's Defense Policy: Other Views" (Mar. 30, 1983), vol. 9, no. 12, p. 5 (transcript on microfilm, Widener Library); Callahan's comment is taken from his article "The Delusion of Defense Again," *America* (Apr. 30, 1983): 341.

7. "The Death-Ray Solution," *Chicago Tribune,* Mar. 26, 1983, sec. 1, p. 6; Russell Baker, "Space Wars," *Atlanta Constitution,* Apr. 4, 1983, p. 15A; "Price Tag for 'Star Wars,' " *St. Louis Post-Dispatch,* Oct. 22, 1983, p. 4A; "In Pursuit of Icarus," *New York Times,* Dec. 4, 1983, sec. 4, p. E20; Daniel S. Greenberg, " 'Star Wars'—An X-Rated Misadventure," *Los Angeles Times,* Nov. 13, 1983, p. 5; Art Buchwald, "Star Wars for Bonzo," *Washington Post,* Apr. 5, 1983, p. C1.

8. William A. Gamson, "Reframing the Debate: The Struggle for Peace and Disarmament Is a Struggle over Language and Perception," *Nuclear Times* 5, no. 5 (July/Aug. 1987): 27. Philip M. Boffey noted the popularity of "initiative" in a variety of other programs: the Superconductive Initiative, the Strategic Computing Initiative, the Air Defense Initiative (to cope with threats that missile defense could not), the Conventional Defense Initiative, the Caribbean Basin Initiative, and so on. See Boffey, "Brimming with Initiative," *New York Times,* July 29, 1987, p. D23. I refer to the president's proposal as the Grand Vision, and I also speak more generally about "missile defense" because until the spring of 1984 there was no official name for the project. I use the acronym SDI, which refers to the official name given to the Vision, but I do not necessarily accept the package of assumptions that comes with such use.

9. Kennedy is quoted in "Glossary: 'Star Wars,' " *Boston Globe,* Jan. 21, 1985, p. 18. Reportedly, he accused the president of "misleading Red Scare tactics and reckless Star Wars schemes." Sellers is quoted in Ron Martz, "SDI Advocate Goes to Battle over Negative 'Star Wars' Image," *Atlanta Journal and Constitution,* Dec. 29, 1985, p. 22. Wilson calls attention to his earlier use of the term in "How Reagan's 'Star Wars' Got Its Name," *Boston Globe,* Jan. 27, 1985, p. A27; and see his article "Make Way, Please, for Star Wars," ibid., Mar. 8, 1982, p. 11. See also "No Need for Star Wars," *Mother Jones* (Aug. 1980): 10.

10. The president's remarks are in "Strategic Defense Initiative," *Weekly Compilation of Presidential Documents* 21, no. 11 (Mar. 18, 1985): 279. See also "Star Wars and Broken Treaties," *The Phyllis Schlafly Report* 18, no. 4, sec. 1 (Nov. 1984): 1. Jack Stevens's comment was made during an interview with the author, Mar. 12, 1987.

11. William Safire, "Acronym Sought," *New York Times Magazine* (Feb. 24, 1985): 10. The responses are from Safire, "New Name for 'Star Wars,' " ibid. (Mar. 24, 1985): 15-16.

12. Ashton Carter, *Directed Energy Missile Defense in Space* (Washington, D.C.: U.S. Congress, Office of Technology Assessment, Apr. 1984), 81; Tom Wicker, "Two Spacey Schemes," *New York Times,* May 11, 1984, p. A31; "A Report to Heed," *St. Louis Post-Dispatch,* Mar. 24, 1984, p. 10A. In October 1985, John Bosma, defense policy adviser to Rep. Ken Kramer (R., Colo.), accused OTA of being a captive think tank of the Democratic party. See Bosma, "Arms Control, SDI, and the Geneva Conventions," in Zbigniew Brzezinski, ed., *Promise or Peril: The Strategic Defense Initiative* (Washington, D.C.: Ethics and Public Policy Center, 1986), 362. For a history of the SDIO, see Ruth Currie McDaniel, *The U.S. Army Strategic Defense Command: Its History and Role in the Strategic Defense Initiative* (n.p.: Historical Office, U.S. Army Strategic Defense Command, 2d ed., 1987); see also *Strategic Defense Initiative: A Chronology, 1983-1988* (Washington, D.C.: U.S. Arms Control and Disarmament Agency, 1988).

13. "15 Years of UCS," *Nucleus* (Spring 1984): 3; *Wall Street Journal,* Dec. 10, 1984, p. 26; William Rusher, "The End of Horror," *High Frontier Newsletter* 1, no. 12 (June/July 1984): 2; "Space Defense and Its Attackers," *National Review* (Feb. 22, 1985): 16. Gregory A. Fossedal, former editorial writer at the *Wall Street Journal* and subsequently a fellow at the Hoover Institute, remarked that UCS was the "principal custodian of the perverse logic of

mutual assured destruction." See Fossedal, "Beware of the Union Label: The Metaphysics and Politics of the UCS," *Policy Review* 32 (Spring 1985): 47.

14. Robert Jastrow, *How to Make Nuclear Weapons Obsolete* (Boston: Little, Brown & Co., 1985). For Jastrow's comments on anti-SDI scientists, see "Reagan vs. the Scientists," *Commentary* 77, no. 1 (Jan. 1984): 23-32; "The War against 'Star Wars,' " ibid. 78, no. 6 (Dec. 1984): 19-25. See also Jastrow, "Why We Need 'Star Wars,' " *Reader's Digest* (Feb. 1986): 2-6; "Dim Prospects for SDI," *National Review* (Aug. 15, 1986): 14. For Garwin's thoughts, see Union of Concerned Scientists, *The Fallacy of Star Wars* (New York: Vintage Books, 1984); Hans A. Bethe, Jeffrey Boutwell, and Richard Garwin, "BMD Technologies and Concepts in the 1980's" in *Weapons in Space,* vol. 1: *Concepts and Technologies* (*Daedalus* 114, no. 2 [Spring 1985]), 53-71; response to Jastrow in "Star Wars: Robert Jastrow and Critics," *Commentary* 77, no. 6 (June 1984): 4-5. See also John Tirman, "Walking Out of Star Wars," *Esquire* (Oct. 1984): 110-20.

15. "Scientists at the White House," *Science* 227 (Mar. 1, 1985): 1015; John Kogut and Michael Weissman, "Taking the Pledge against Star Wars," *Bulletin of the Atomic Scientists* 42, no. 1 (Jan. 1986): 28.

16. Lisbeth Gronlud, John Kogut, Michael Weissman, and David Wright, "A Status Report on the Boycott of Star Wars Research by Academic Scientists and Engineers," May 13, 1986, p. 2 (author's files); Union of Concerned Scientists, "1985 Annual Report," p. 3 (author's files); see also Wayne Biddle, "Scientists Compare 'Star Wars' to ABM Debates," *New York Times,* May 30, 1985, p. B6; Jeffrey Smith, "Caltech, MIT Deny Role in Star Wars Research," *Science* 228 (June 21, 1985): 1411.

17. Ionson quoted in "Campuses' Role in Arms Debated as 'Star Wars' Funds Are Sought," *New York Times,* July 22, 1985, p. 1; Gregory A. Fossedal, "Star Wars and the Scientists," *Wall Street Journal,* June 14, 1985, p. 24. Hoffert and Herman quoted in *Washington Times,* May 12, 1986; see also "Scientists' 'Star Wars' Protests Not Likely to Cripple Program," *Los Angeles Times,* May 29, 1986, sec. 1, p. 20.

18. Karl O'Lessker, "More "Masked Politics' from Anti-SDI Scientists," *Wall Street Journal,* August 1, 1985, p. 16; John Hughes, "Against Research?," *Christian Science Monitor,* Sept. 20, 1985, p. 14; Science and Engineering Committee for a Secure World, printed material (author's files).

19. Gronlund et al., "Status Report," 9, 11. In addition, there were scattered public attempts to mock serious scientific efforts to create missile defense. On March 23, 1986, for example, the Colorado STARS committee held a "Lemon Day," designed to spoof SDI; that same spring, students at the California Institute of Technology held their second annual contest to come up with defense proposals as "outlandish" as SDI. For a description of Cal Tech's contest, see "Inflated Hippos Touted in Star Wars Lampoon," *Houston Post,* May 17, 1986, p. 7C.

CHAPTER 2

1. Kevin Phillips, "Defense beyond Thin Air: Space Holds the Audience," *Los Angeles Times,* Mar. 10, 1985, sec. 4, p. 3.

2. The first and third quotes are from "High Frontier: A New Option in

Space," *National Security Record* (June 1982): 1; Graham's remark is in Graham, *The Case for Space Defense* (Louisville, Ky.: Frank Simon Co., 1986), 31.

3. "How to Wage a Successful Summit," *The Phyllis Schlafly Report* 19, no. 6, sec. 1 (Jan. 1986): 3. Henry Kissinger offered a much more sophisticated version of this argument, focusing not on postwar liberal elites but on the enervating effects of nuclear anxiety on the general public. SDI was a good idea, he said, because "democratic peoples will sooner or later retreat to pacifism and unilateral disarmament." Kissinger, "We Need Star Wars," *Washington Post,* Sept. 8, 1985, p. C8. See also "Why Are Liberals Opposed to a Strong American Presence in Space: An Interview with Congressman Newt Gingrich," pamphlet, American Space Federation, n.d.; William Rusher, "The End of Horror," *High Frontier Newsletter* 1, no. 12 (June/July 1984): 2; Daniel O. Graham, *We Must Defend America and Put an End to MADness* (Chicago: Regnery Gateway, 1983), 24.

4. "The Best Defense Is a Good Defense," *Detroit News,* Jan. 23, 1985, p. 12A; George Keyworth, "Ganging Up on Star Wars," *Washington Post,* Dec. 24, 1984, p. A15; William F. Buckley, "Trading SDI," ibid., Aug. 22, 1986, p. A19.

5. Michael L. Smith, "Selling the Moon: The U.S. Manned Space Program and the Triumph of Commodity Scientism," in Richard Wrightman Fox and T. J. Jackson Lears, eds., *The Culture of Consumption: Critical Essays in American History, 1880-1980* (New York: Pantheon Books, 1983), 177. Excerpts from the president's speech are in *High Frontier Newsletter* 1, no. 12, (June/July 1984): 5; see also Graham, *The Case for Space Defense,* 10.

6. *Houston Post,* Jan. 29, 1986, p. 2A; "Reagan Says Explosion Strengthens Resolve," *Boston Globe,* Jan. 31, 1986, p. 62.

7. An insightful discussion of the symbol of fate in the nuclear age can be found in Ira Chernus, *Dr. Strangegod: On the Symbolic Meaning of Nuclear Weapons* (Columbia: University of South Carolina Press, 1986), 53-62. The quotes are from David Hoffman, "Reagan Firm on 'Star Wars' Research," *Boston Globe,* July 13, 1986, p. 1; Citizens for America, "Call for Action," Oct. 28, 1985 (letter in author's files).

8. Weinberger's exchange with Kalb is in Arms Control Association, comps., *Star Wars Quotes* (Washington, D.C.: Arms Control Association, July 1986), 51; Richard Sybert, "Reagan's Strategic Defense Initiative," *Los Angeles Times,* Nov. 2, 1985, sec. 2, p. 2.

9. See William K. Wyant, "GOP Charges That U.S. Trails Russia in Missile Defense," *St. Louis Post-Dispatch,* Feb. 21, 1967, and "Missile Defense Shaping Up as GOP Right Wing Issue," ibid., Feb. 26, 1967; American Security Council, *USSR vs. USA: The ABM Debate and the Changed Strategic Military Balance* (Washington, D.C.: Acropolis Books, 1969), 10.

10. Transcript of "This Week with David Brinkley," ABC News, no. 128, Apr. 8, 1984, p. 4; "Red Star Wars," *Wall Street Journal,* Apr. 10, 1985, p. 28; Ralph K. Bennett, "Russia's Red Shield," *Reader's Digest* (July 1986): 4; "Soviet's First Strike Arsenal Backed Up by 'Dark Star' ABM Defense," *Defense Watch* (Jan./Feb. 1987): 1, 6; D. James Kennedy, *Surviving the Nuclear Age* (Fort Lauderdale, Fla.: Coral Ridge Ministries, n.d.), 7.

11. "Update on News," *Concerned Women for America Newsletter* 9, no. 1 (Dec. 1986/Jan. 1987): 10; Citizens for America, "Sample Field Op-Ed,"

Oct. 29, 1986 (author's files). High Frontier also saw calamitous results emerging from Soviet missile defense. According to Daniel Graham, the United States was facing the new era of " 'Pax Sovietica' in which Soviet space power dictates Free World behavior." Graham, *High Frontier: A New National Strategy* (Washington, D.C.: Heritage Foundation, 1982), 3.

12. Kramer's remark is in Larry Pressler, *Star Wars: The Strategic Defense Debates in Congress* (New York: Praeger, 1986), 67; Weinberger's comment was made on "Meet the Press," NBC News, Mar. 27, 1983 (transcript in author's files). See also "Star Wars" (letter to the editor), *Christian Science Monitor,* Dec. 10, 1985, p. 29.

13. "H-Bomb/SDI Debates and the Scientists: Will It Work," Republican Study Committee, Apr. 4, 1986, printed material (author's files).

14. For the Abrahamson and Weinberger quotes, see "This Week with David Brinkley," Apr. 8, 1984, pp. 3, 7 (transcript in author's files). See also John A. Farrell, "New Space Boss Assails Critics of 'Star Wars' Plan," *Denver Post,* Nov. 28, 1984, p. 3A; "Why Moscow Fears 'Star Wars,' " *National Security Record* 78 (Apr. 1985): 5.

15. Norman Podhoretz, "And Betray Their Profession," *Minneapolis Star and Tribune,* June 11, 1985, p. A10; "Physicists: Laser Shield Could Be on Line by 2000," *Houston Post,* Aug. 22, 1984, p. 2A.

16. W. Bruce Weinrod, ed., *Assessing Strategic Defense: Six Roundtable Discussions* (Washington, D.C.: Heritage Foundation, 1985), vii; Science and Engineering Committee for a Secure World, pamphlet, May 1986 (author's files). Such optimism regarding futuristic weapons was not new. For example, in 1961 *Electronics* reported that Martin Marietta was developing a laser "capable of beaming a million degree ray . . . to vaporize hostile space weapons." See Mark H. Maier and Thomas J. Venanzi, "Return of the Death Ray: The Star Wars Defense Plan Is a Costly Remake of an Old Fantasy," *Sciences* 25, no. 2 (1985): 32.

17. Robert Jastrow, "Dim Prospects for SDI," *National Review* (Aug. 15, 1986): 14; Kennedy, *Surviving the Nuclear Age,* 9; *Concerned Women for America Newsletter* 8, no. 11 (Nov. 1986): 15.

18. "Star Wars Works," *Wall Street Journal,* June 25, 1984; "It Can Be Done," *Forbes* (July 16, 1984): 30; Jack Anderson, *New York Times,* Oct. 29, 1984, p. A23.

19. Republican Study Committee, "SDI: The Need for Near-Term Deployment," pamphlet, July 18, 1986, p. 3 (author's files).

20. For a good introduction to the history of the development of Soviet missile defense, see David Holloway, "The Strategic Defense Initative and the Soviet Union," in *Weapons in Space,* vol. 2: *Implications for Security (Daedalus* 114, no. 3 [Summer 1985]), 257-78; William J. Broad, "The Secrets of Soviet Star Wars," *New York Times Magazine* (June 28, 1987): 22ff.

21. Gregory Fossedal, in "A Bipartisan Memo on Star Wars," *Wall Street Journal,* Aug. 17, 1984, p. 14, called for antinuclear activists to join SDI supporters in promoting missile defense as a way to transcend their differences. He claimed that Jonathan Schell, author of the widely read antinuclear book *The Fate of the Earth,* had seen the wisdom of missile defense and was becoming an SDI supporter. Like so much of Fossedal's writing on SDI, there is only a half-truth here. In *The Abolition,* Schell argued that defensive weapons

might make sense *after* all nuclear weapons are destroyed. Of the president's Vision, Schell said that "the order of events in his proposal was wrong. If we seek first to defend ourselves, and not to abolish nuclear weapons until after we have made that effort, we will never abolish them . . . because of the irreversible superiority of the offensive in the nuclear world." Schell, *The Abolition* (New York: Avon Books, 1986), 149.

22. Stephen S. Rosenfeld, "A Dizzying Strategy," *Washington Post,* Feb. 1, 1985, p. A19.

23. Barry J. Smernoff, "Images of the Nuclear Future," *Air University Review* 34 (May/June 1983): 8, 10; Caspar W. Weinberger, "Ethics and Public Policy," *The Fletcher Forum* 10, no. 1 (Winter 1986): 1; Weinberger, "Strategic Defense Initiative: Creating Options for a Safer World," *Los Angeles Times,* July 9, 1985, sec. 2, p. 5; Lewis Lehrman, "A Moral Case for 'Star Wars,' " *New York Times,* Feb. 19, 1985, p. A23.

24. Coalition for the Strategic Defense Initiative, clergy statement (author's files); "Religious Leaders and Groups Endorse 'Star Wars' as 'Moral Policy,' " ad hoc Religious Coalition for a Moral Defense Policy, Feb. 4, 1986, news release (author's files); National Association of Evangelicals, *Guidelines: Peace, Freedom and Security Studies* (Wheaton, Ill.: National Association of Evangelicals, 1986), 28. Pat Robertson, who had been an enthusiastic supporter of SDI during his tenure at the Christian Broadcasting Network, continued his support during his campaign for the Republican nomination for president: "I am in favor of SDI's earliest possible deployment and against relegating SDI to 'bargaining chip' status." See Council for a Livable World Education Fund and Freeze Voter Education Fund, *Nuclear Arms Control and the 1988 Presidential Candidates* (Boston: Council for a Livable World Education Fund, 1988), 29. Missile defense was also presented as the only moral alternative to the dangers of the nuclear age in the National Council for Better Education's secondary-level curriculum for social studies, *The Strategy of Defense* (Alexandria, Va.: National Council for Better Education, n.d.). The council was formed to counteract the programs of liberals, who have "dominated and controlled American education for years" (NCBE brochure, author's files).

25. Patricia S. Lefevere, "Peace Pastoral Influenced Star Wars, Contends Reagan Advisor," *National Catholic Reporter* (May 10, 1945): 2; Joseph Martino, " 'Star Wars'—Technology's New Challenge to Moralists," *This World* 9 (Fall 1984): 15-29; Kenneth W. Kemp, "The Moral Case for the Strategic Defense Initiative," *Catholicism in Crisis* (June 1985): 22; George Weigel, *Tranquillitas Ordinis: The Present Failure and Future Promise of American Catholic Thought on War and Peace* (New York: Oxford University Press, 1987); Philip F. Lawler, *The Ultimate Weapon* (Chicago: Regnery Gateway, 1984), 101.

26. Kennedy, *Surviving the Nuclear Age,* 10: "Network of Prayer and Action," *Concerned Women for America Newsletter* 8, no. 11 (Nov. 1986): 3; Moore's letter to the *New York Times,* Mar. 17, 1986, p. A18; Ronald Reagan, "Strategic Defense Initiative: Radio Address to the Nation," *Weekly Compilation of Presidential Documents* 21 (July 22, 1985): 901-2.

27. Weinberger, "Ethics and Public Policy," 6. During a speaking engagement with the SDIO working group of the National Security Council on June 29, 1987, I was struck by how deeply some supporters felt about the moral ar-

guments. Several members of the group spoke of the perfect symmetry between the moral requirements of defense in the nuclear age and the characteristics of SDI. I felt a sense of "injured innocence" in the group, a genuine puzzlement that such a morally superior (in their view) program could generate such fierce opposition.

28. "The Road to Star Wars," *Wall Street Journal,* Mar. 27, 1984, p. 34; Colin S. Gray, "Controversy over 'Star Wars,'" *Christian Science Monitor,* Aug. 9, 1985, p. A16.

29. Armand Hammer, "Sharing 'Star Wars,'" *New York Times,* Sept. 22, 1985, sec. 1, p. E21; Jacob K. Javits, "Let's Help Moscow—and Ourselves," *New York Times,* Jan. 26, 1986, sec. 4, p. E21.

30. The speech was delivered on February 6, 1985; for the text, see "Is the Administration's 'Star Wars' Strategic Defense Initiative Sound National Policy?," *Congressional Digest* 64 (Mar. 1985): 65-68; Robert B. Reich, "High-Tech, a Subsidiary of Pentagon, Inc.," *New York Times,* May 29, 1985, p. A23. See also Malcolm W. Browne, "The Star Wars Spinoff," *New York Times Magazine* (Aug. 24, 1986): 19-20ff.

31. Edward Teller, *Better a Shield Than a Sword* (New York: Free Press, 1987), 26.

32. Phyllis Schlafly, "We Must Deploy SDI Now," *The Phyllis Schlafly Report* 20, no. 6, sec. 1 (Jan. 1987). For comparisons to a gas mask, see "Strategic Defense Initiative," *Weekly Compilation of Presidential Documents* 21, no. 11 (Mar. 18, 1985): 281; "Fantasy as History," *St. Louis Post-Dispatch,* Feb. 13, 1985, p. 7A; "Star Wars: Vanity and Reality," *New York Times,* Sept. 19, 1985, p. A34. The president's "fort" statements can be found in Gerald M. Boyd, "President Is Critical of 'Liberals' Who May 'Chop Up' 'Star Wars,'" *New York Times,* Oct. 19, 1986, p. A10; "Reagan Injects Arm Shield Issue onto Campaign Trail," *Boston Globe,* Oct. 16, 1986, p. 23. Weinberger's statement is found in Clement Dixon, "Star Wars: The Administration Strikes Back," *Defense Science* (June 1983): 11. See also Vermont Royster, "'Star Wars' or MADness," *Wall Street Journal,* Jan. 30, 1985, p. 26; Malcolm S. Forbes, Jr., "Can He Save SDI?," *Forbes* 138 (Sept. 8, 1986): 23.

33. Phillips, "Defense beyond Thin Air."

CHAPTER 3

1. Townsend Hoopes, "'Star Wars'—A Way of Going It Alone but We Live Together—or Perish Together," *New York Times,* Jan. 2, 1986, p. A19. Oppenheimer is quoted in Lawrence Freedman, *The Evolution of Nuclear Strategy* (New York: St. Martin's Press, 1981), 94.

2. Schlesinger is quoted in Tom Wicker, "Informing the People," *New York Times,* Oct. 4, 1985, p. A31. For similar pronouncements, see Harrison Brown, "Star Wars Once Funny, Now Frightening," *Bulletin of the Atomic Scientists* 41, no. 5 (May 1985): 3; Wolfgang Panofsky, "'Star Wars' Isn't a Science Yet," *Los Angeles Times,* July 11, 1985, sec. 2, p. 5.

3. "ABC News Nightline: SDI: Windfall or Payoff," no. 1296, May 12, 1986, p. 5 (transcript in author's files). Even some people involved in the program were bothered by the heady optimism. George H. Miller, head of defensive programs at Lawrence Livermore Laboratory, said, "I'm very alarmed at the degree of hype, promises, and a failure to focus on what this national program

really is—a research program with lots of unanswered questions." Quoted in William Broad, "Science Showmanship: A Deep 'Star Wars' Rift," *New York Times,* Dec. 16, 1985, p. A1.

4. George Rathjens and Jack Ruina, "BMD and Strategic Instability," in *Weapons in Space,* vol. 2: *Implications for Security (Daedalus* 114, no. 3 [Summer 1985]), 255.

5. Paul Boyer, "How S.D.I. Will Change Our Culture," *The Nation* (Jan. 10, 1987): 17.

6. E. P. Thompson, ed., *Star Wars: Science Fiction Fantasy or Serious Possibility?* (Harmondsworth, U.K.: Penguin Books, 1985), 3; Thompson, "The Real Meaning of Star Wars," *The Nation* (Mar. 9, 1985): 275; "The Star Wars Scenario, One Year Later," *Christianity and Crisis* (May 14, 1984): 172; Erwin Knoll, "The Biggest Lie," *Progressive* 47, no. 5 (May 1983): 9. See also Robert E. Hunter, " 'Star Wars' and Modern Realities," *Los Angeles Times,* Feb. 14, 1985, sec. 2, p. 5; "Buck Rogers in the 14th Century," *Christianity and Crisis* (Apr. 18, 1983): 131-32.

7. "Zero Defect," *Boston Globe,* Aug. 6, 1985, p. 12; Nicholas Wade, "Second Chances in Space," *New York Times,* Aug. 9, 1985, p. A26.

8. James Reston, "Where Are We Going?," *New York Times,* Feb. 2, 1986, p. E21; *Philadephia Inquirer,* Feb. 2, 1986, p. 9-G; "Star Wars Danger," *America* (Mar. 8, 1986): 178.

9. William F. Buckley, Jr., *New Orleans Times-Picayune,* Feb. 22, 1986, p. A19; Phyllis Schlafly, "We Must Deploy SDI Now," *The Phyllis Schlafly Report* 20, no. 6, sec. 1 (Jan. 1987): 3.

10. Ellen Goodman, "A 'Dream' Called Star Wars," *Washington Post,* May 13, 1986, p. A19; Anthony Lewis, "Silent Spring: The Meaning of Chernobyl Is Very Clear in the Italian Countryside," *New York Times,* May 29, 1986, p. A23; J. Bennett Johnston, "Chernobyls in Space?," *Washington Post,* June 8, 1986, p. F7.

11. Schlafly, "We Must Deploy SDI Now," p. 1.

12. "The False Promise of ABM," *St. Louis Post-Dispatch,* June 14, 1984, p. 20A; E. R. Heiberg III, "A Bull's Eye for the Army," *Wall Street Journal,* July 5, 1984, p. 15.

13. Joseph S. Nye, Jr., "[The] Only Test of SDI Morality Will Be Its Consequences," *Los Angeles Times,* June 5, 1986, sec. 2, p. 7. For Nye's discussion of general questions of morality in relation to nuclear weapons, see *Nuclear Ethics* (New York: Free Press, 1986). See also David Heim, "Starry-eyed over Star Wars," *Christian Century* (Feb. 19, 1983): 165.

14. "Stop Space Weapons: Resume Space Cooperation," 1984 General Assembly of the Unitarian Universalist Association, printed material (author's files); "We Have No Faith in Star Wars," American Friends Service Committee, May 10, 1985, printed material (author's files); "Church Group Puts Own Control Plan into Arms Arena," *St. Louis Post-Dispatch,* Aug. 1, 1985, p. 2B; "Responding to the Development of Space Weaponry," Fifteenth General Synod of the United Church of Christ, 1985, printed material (author's files); "A Message Concerning Arms Negotiations Following the Reagan-Gorbachev Meeting at Reykjavik," National Council of the Churches of Christ in the U.S.A., Nov. 6, 1986, printed material (author's files); "Resolution on the

Militarization of Space," 198th General Assembly of the Presbyterian Church, U.S.A., 1986, printed material (author's files).

15. United Methodists Council of Bishops, *In Defense of Creation: The Nuclear Crisis and a Just Peace* (Nashville: Graded Press, 1986), 52; Robert Jewett, "A Covenant with Death," *Christian Century* (May 18, 1983): 477; Danny Collum and Jim Rice, "To Tell the Truth: Will the Real SDI Please Stand Up?," *Sojourners* 16, no. 5 (May 1987): 17. The activities of "Peace Pentecost" are highlighed in ibid., p. 25.

16. Robert F. Drinan, "Star Wars Leap Could Escalate the Arms Race," *National Catholic Reporter* 19 (May 6, 1983): 21; "S.D.I. and the 'Challenge of Peace,' " *America* 153 (Nov. 23, 1985): 338.

17. All the statements from Bernardin and O'Connor are taken from U.S. Congress, House, Committee on Foreign Affairs, *The Role of Arms Control in U.S. Defense Policy: Hearings before the Committee on Foreign Affairs,* 98th Cong., 2d sess., 1984, pp. 131-35. For a report on the speech Bernardin prepared for the University of Missouri at Columbia, see Bruce Bursma, "Bernardin Takes Aim at 'Star Wars' Plan," *Chicago Tribune,* Mar. 8, 1985, sec. 1, p. 20. In 1987, after several years of study of the pastoral letter, a committee of Roman Catholic bishops concluded that deterrence was not a satisfactory long-term method of keeping the peace and that SDI research should only proceed within the confines of the ABM treaty and not be "pressed to deployment." See "U.S. Catholic Bishops on Nuclear Deterrence," *New York Times,* Apr. 15, 1988, p. A18; Peter Steinfels, "U.S. Bishops Oppose Anti-Missile Plan," ibid.

18. Spark M. Matsunaga, "U.S.-Soviet Space Cooperation and Arms Control," *Bulletin of the Atomic Scientists* 41, no. 3 (Mar. 1985): 19. Kennedy is quoted by Rep. John J. Moakley (D., Mass.) in "The 'Star Wars' Controversy: Pro & Con," *Congressional Digest* 64 (Mar. 1985): 89.

19. U.S. Congress, House, Committee on Foreign Affairs, *Arms Control in Outer Space: Hearings before a Subcommitte on International Security and Science,* 98th Cong., 1st and 2d sess., 1984, p. 2; "Cooperative East-West Ventures," Public Law 98-562, *U.S. Code Congressional and Administrative News,* 2, 98th Cong., 2d sess., 1984, vol. 2, 98 stat., 2914 and 2915; U.S. Congress, House, Committee on Foreign Affairs, *East-West Cooperation in Outer Space,* p. 9.

20. "Before a Mission to Mars," *St. Louis Post-Dispatch,* Sept. 18, 1984, p. 2B; Jack Kidd, "Star Light Can Be an Alternative to Star Wars," *Humanist* 45 (Sept./Oct. 1985): 28. For a detailed "Star Trek" program of possible superpower space cooperation, see Daniel Deudney, "Forging Weapons into Spaceships," *World Policy Journal* (Spring 1985); comment on these programs is in *New York Times,* Nov. 12, 1986, p. 24. Not all memories of past superpower cooperation in space led to these kinds of alternative visions. Michael Intriligator of UCLA's Center for International and Strategic Affairs thought the memory of Apollo-Soyuz could very well point the way to a "partnership" in the construction of a limited SDI by each nation. See Intriligator, "Why Not a 'Star Wars' Partnership?," *Los Angeles Times,* Oct. 20, 1985, sec. 4, p. 5.

21. Patricia Mische, *Star Wars and the State of Our Souls* (Minneapolis: Winston Press, 1985), p. 113 and passim.

22. See, for example, "Transcript of the Reagan-Mondale Debate on Foreign Policy," *New York Times,* Oct. 22, 1986, p. B6.

23. Daniel O. Graham, Mar. 11, 1986, interview with the author. Alvin Richman, a senior public opinion analyst for the State Department observed that a November 1986 G. Lawrence poll found that "the *least* persuasive of six arguments against SDI . . . was that 'SDI won't work.' " See Richman, "Gauging the American Public's Attitudes toward SDI from National Polls," paper delivered at the 1987 annual meeting of the International Studies Association, Apr. 15-18, 1987, Washington, D.C. (author's files).

24. *High Frontier Newsletter* 2, no. 1 (Oct. 1984): 5; Flora Lewis, "Fantasy on Film," *New York Times,* Mar., 29, 1985, p. A35.

25. I would like to thank the Union of Concerned Scientists and High Frontier, Inc., for providing me with videotape copies of their respective advertisements.

26. Art Buchwald, "Drawing the Nuclear Line," *Washington Post,* Dec. 10, 1985, p. B1.

27. Ann Cahn is quoted in "Commercial Wars over Star Wars Begins: New TV Spot Counters Pro–Star Wars 'Crayola' Ad: Begins Airing November 13 in D.C. Market," news release, Richard Pollock Associates, Inc., Nov. 12, 1985 (author's files). I would like to thank Richard Pollock Associates for providing me with a videotape copy of "Space Wars I."

28. "Judge Upholds Usage of Phrase 'Star Wars,' " *New York Times,* Nov. 27, 1985, p. B8.

29. Kendall and Graham appeared on "CBS Evening News with Dan Rather" (Nov. 14, 1985), vol. 11, no. 318, p. 8 (transcript on microfilm, Widener Library). See also Richard Stengel, "The Great Star Wars P.R. War: Kindergarten Imagery Obscures a Vital and Complex Debate," *Time* (Dec. 9, 1985): 31-32. High Frontier and UCS have also produced half-hour and hour-length educational videotapes about SDI.

Index

A Note on the Author

EDWARD TABOR LINENTHAL is a professor of religious studies at the University of Wisconsin at Oshkosh. He has been affiliated with the Defense and Arms Control Studies Program at the Massachusetts Institute of Technology, as a research fellow, and with the Wisconsin Institute for the Study of War, Peace, and Global Cooperation. He is the author of *Changing Images of the Warrior Hero in America.* His next book will be a study of the cultural significance of American battlefields.